ROUND AND ABOUT THE
BOOK-STALLS.

This Edition is limited to 1,000 copies and is a Facsimile Republication of the original 1891 London Edition.

Published by
Canterbury Bookshop
538 South Wabash Ave.
Chicago, Ill. 60605

ROUND AND ABOUT

THE

BOOK-STALLS.

A GUIDE

FOR THE BOOK-HUNTER.

BY

J. HERBERT SLATER,

Editor of "Book Prices Current"; formerly Editor of "Book-Lore"; Author of "The Library Manual," "Engravings and Their Value," "Book Collecting" ("Young Collector" Series), "The Law Relating to Copyright and Trade Marks," &c.

LONDON:

L. UPCOTT GILL, 170, STRAND, W.C.

1891.

LONDON:

A. BRADLEY, LONDON AND COUNTY PRINTING WORKS,

DRURY LANE, W.C.

LIBRARY OF CONGRESS CARD NUMBER: 74-80834

PREFACE.

THIS is essentially a work for the book-hunter. In it I have endeavoured to point clearly and concisely to those classes of books which are now but little thought of, but which should rise in value in the near future, and also to those books of present value which, though of mean appearance, are likely to be met with on the stalls of the dealers. The principles upon which books of all kinds derive their value and importance are also stated and discussed. In each of these respects the work is, so far as I am aware, unique.

J. H. S.

CROUCH END, N.
March, 1891.

CONTENTS.

CONTENTS

ROUND AND ABOUT THE BOOK-STALLS.

CHAPTER I.

MONEY AND BOOKS.

THE true book-hunter considers himself a discoverer rather than a purchaser, and it is the essence of his skill to find value in those things which in the eye of the ordinary possessor are really worthless. There are obviously many descriptions of book-hunters, for some few at least rely on the depth of their purse rather than on the height of their discretion; others regard their books as so many handsome pieces of furniture, arranged for ornament rather than use; others, again, rejoice in a bargain for the mere love of gain, and trouble themselves not so much with the contents of their books as with speculations on their probable worth and the chance of their increasing in value as time goes on.   As the angler whose patience is fortified with the thoughts of the pecuniary value of his catch, is regarded by his brother Waltonians—that is to say, with derision and contempt—so is the hungry book-hunter who buys to sell again at a profit, and whose whole soul is absorbed in the contemplation of prospective gain.

Let it not be supposed, therefore, that although it is the province of the true book-hunter to find value in those things which in the eye of the ordinary possessor are really worthless, his ambition is grovelling or his hopes mercenary ; on the contrary, the "value" of a book to him lies in the nature of the contents, or perhaps in its history or in that of the man who wrote it, or in the special circumstances which give it an importance and a place upon his shelves.

Don Vincente, a priest of Barcelona, outbidden in a competition for a rare volume, strangled the purchaser in his own house, and by adding arson to murder and theft concealed the crime for many months.   At last he was detected with the missing volume in his possession, and when the Crown advanced as a proof of his guilt the argument that the book was unique—as indeed it was believed to be—his counsel showed that without doubt there was another copy in the Louvre. What said Don Vincente? Did he treat the bibliographical discovery with indifference as being immaterial so far as he was concerned, under the altered circumstances? Quite the contrary, for falling on his knees he exclaimed, " Ah! my error was great indeed: *my copy was not unique.*"

It would require more than the sophistry of Euthydemos to palliate the conduct of Don Vincente, but there is no gainsaying the fact that he was, his barbarities notwithstanding, a true lover of books. Though no crime was too atrocious for him to commit, it may be more than doubted whether he would have aped the thief who stole a transcript of the " De Consolatione " of Boethius, " the last of the classics " as it has been called, from the Vatican, and within a few hours sold it to another library at Rome. We could easily credit him with the theft, but with a vulgar sale, never—unless indeed the purchaser had yielded up the book with his speedy death, as happened in one or two other instances in which Don Vincente was suspected of being concerned.

Let not, however, lovers of books protest against any fancied resemblance between themselves and the renegade Spanish priest, for no such comparison is possible. Their affection will prompt to no more inconvenient act than that of the old bookseller mentioned by Lord Lytton, who having parted from sheer necessity with a valued book from among his stock, paced all night in the cold and damp before the house of the envied purchaser, repenting bitterly that the pangs of hunger should have so warped his soul.

Thus it is with all genuine book-lovers, over whom the inevitable hour of parting hangs like a cloud, and to whom each particular volume within reach seems to say, "I was another's yesterday; to-day I am yours; to-morrow and you will see me again no more."

Between the lover of books for their own sake and the mere book-hunter there is indeed a wide distinction, and the former perhaps needs to be reminded occasionally that there is such a thing as trade in books, and that there are plenty of genuine book-hunters who will without compunction send whole rows of life's companions to the block. Such as they never buy a book without weighing the price, and if the object is to gather together a representative assortment of volumes, the element of value, present or prospective, is continually associated with the collection.

With the book-lover the case is different, for although he may in all prudence have husbanded his resources originally, the question of pecuniary value is for ever after eliminated from his mind. These two classes of bookmen have little in common, and each views the other with feelings akin to pity. The one regards the worldling as sordid, and a man without heart; while he, on his part, looks upon his more enthusiastic rival as a dry-as-dust.

"All my friends," says a recent writer, "must bear about them a literary flavour, however faint: if they have a delicate appreciation of poetry, so much the better shall I be pleased. They should be bookish to some degree, for otherwise our conversation would be wanting in its finest points, our sympathy slight, and the rush of soul to soul altogether absent. They must know more than the outsides of the volumes they claim acquaintance with, and infinitely more than their catalogue prices. If a friend exhibits with reasonable pride, say a clean uncut copy of 'The Lives and Characters of the English Dramatic Poets' . . . I share his pride with him; but to please me as I wish to be pleased, he should have knowledge of the curiosities to be found within its covers. Let him know that Sir William d'Avenant was 'the son of John d'Avenant, vintner of Oxford, in that very house that has now the sign of the crown, near Carfax—a house much frequented by Shakespeare in his frequent journeys to Warwickshire,' concerning which frequenting our author says : ' Whether for the beautiful mistress of the house or the good wine, I shall not determine ;' and that he, the said William d'Avenant, wrote several plays, one of which, ' The Law Against Lovers,' a tragi-comedy, was 'taken from two plays of Shake-speare, viz., *Measure for Measure* and *Much Ado about Nothing*, the language much amended and polished by our author': let my would-be friend but know these facts concerning d'Ave-nant, especially that he 'amended and polished' poor Shakespeare's language, and he establishes my interest in himself, and shall, if only for an evening, share with me the comfort of my study and the companionship of my books."

What would such a dreamer, if he will pardon the word as being uttered in no unfriendly or objectionable sense, say of the conduct of that man who would, while knowing as much about "The Lives and Characters of the English Dra-matic Poets" as he does himself, part with it— not to satisfy the pangs of hunger, as did Lord Lytton's bookseller, but because, like Gallio, he "cared for none of those things"?

What to such a man the Vintner of Oxford and Sir William d'Avenant's polished verse, or the pretty mistress of the "Crown" near Carfax ? What in this book more than, or indeed as much

as, can be read every day for a shilling in the
divine pages of that same William Shakespeare
who made the " Crown " his house of call, whether
on account of a fair face or the quality of the
wine is now immaterial ?   Why dreamily doze
over what has long ago been learned by heart ?
Why treasure even a " clean uncut copy " of
" The Lives and Characters of the English Dra-
matic Poets," which from almost every point of
view except a sentimental one is of but little
importance ?

Thus are the characters of two typical book-
men displayed in words which one has uttered
and the other perhaps often thought. Each pursue
different paths : they part almost at the outset
of a literary life and meet afterwards only
occasionally, and then in competition for some
long-coveted volume which both would like
to have, though for very different reasons.

On this platform of rivalry the spectator takes
his stand, and if he is a good judge of character,
either naturally or by reason of a close acquaint-
anceship with the pages of Lavater, the great
master of a decaying art, he will find much to
amuse and instruct him.   The ardent book-lover,
touched though ever so faintly with the spirit
which pervades the whole craft, can no more
conceal his anxiety than could the French biblio-
phile whose purse gave out just at the hour of

triumph. Shaking his fist across the table, and almost in the face of his antagonist, he shouted, "Never mind : I will have it at your sale"; and history records that he did, for his poor brother died within the year.

There was indeed in this scene more of instruction than amusement, and I cannot help thinking that the lesson to be learned was that it is far better to be tinged even with the spirit of mere vulgar trade than to be saturated with the selfish eagerness of the bibliomaniac.

This, however, is after all a question for the moralist, and affects but in the slightest degree the great book market, which is regulated, not by the whims and fancies or even by the cravings of individuals, but rather by the fiat of the mass.

This fiat goes forth at intervals. It distributes itself into rules, and binds the typical book-hunter, no matter of what description, as with bands of iron, so that in his journeyings round and about the book-stalls he is constrained, though perhaps against his reason, to judge as he knows the vast majority of his fellows would judge under similar circumstances.

It is this unison of thought which controls the market and makes it possible to survey its ups and downs regardless alike of enthusiasm on the one hand or of indifference on the other.

Book-men, of every kind, whether maniacs like Don Vincente, lovers of choice editions like Grolier in France or Beckford in England, readers like Dr. Johnson, Dibdin, or Lamb—the last of whom was once seen to kiss a copy of Chapman's Homer which he had just picked up for a trifle; collectors of the type ridiculed long ago by Seneca as being possessed only of a vulgar emulation which prompted them to accumulate volumes of which, he says, they know nothing except the outsides, many of them possibly barely that: all these sorts and conditions of men, no matter how learned or ignorant, how enthusiastic or indifferent, meet in rivalry on every occasion in which a book is to be bought and sold.

In the great book world as in every other, there is power in wealth, and he whose means are limited must buy in the cheapest market, remembering always what he owes, not merely to himself, but to those who will some day read, or perhaps even be compelled to sell, what he has accumulated with such energy and toil. It is to these that the following pages appeal.

CHAPTER II.

THE GOLDEN DAYS.

THE quality of a people is mirrored in its current literature, and as that is in the main grave or gay, learned or frivolous, just in the same degree is the character of those who support its existence with their money or their applause.

Nothing at first sight seems so easy to gauge by an application of this rule as the popular character at any period of time, nor would there be any difficulty in doing so if the course of the demand for books of a certain class flowed in a single current. Just, however, as the river which we see making its way to the ocean is swollen with innumerable streams and rivulets, so the popular taste in the matter of literature is composed of a vast array of individual preferences. These must be separated, analysed, and classed before any idea can be grasped of the magnitude which would be assumed by a social history founded upon books.

From a practical point of view, there are good reasons why it should be clearly understood at the outset that no book was ever yet sent into the world without an audience, and that the success or the reverse of every literary venture indicates to a nicety the popular taste of the hour, or the phase of it to which the class of work appeals. Attempts are made every day to anticipate results in this respect: some of them succeed, the majority fail, but all afford valuable evidence for future guidance.

The publication of new books is nearly always dominated by one fixed principle, and that a pecuniary one; the purchase of old books, or books at second hand, may be actuated by a variety of motives, among which, perhaps, the question of money never enters at all. Many persons buy books to read or to consult, and do not trouble themselves with speculating on the probabilities of their rise or fall in the market in the near future or at any distance of time. These are the genuine bibliophiles, who read what they collect and can derive as much pleasure from the perusal of a battered volume, with which no bookseller would encumber his shelves, as the latter-day collector takes in contemplating the bindings of rare editions, kept out of harm's way behind glass doors, and which he bought because they cost money and because he thinks that in ten or a dozen years to come, or perhaps less, the pecuniary value will have increased. This type of bookworm rules the market, and nine-tenths of those who search the costermongers' burrows in Farringdon Road and the New Cut do so in the hope of picking up something which will not shame their judgment when the account comes to be balanced. I would not be so unjust as to suggest that books acquired from such a motive are never read : some of them doubtless are—many are not; most are merely skimmed, and then put away out of the reach of dust and dirt and the fingers of the unappreciative.

The quality of this class of collectors, like that of every other, is mirrored in what is to them current literature. The books they hunt after so laboriously, and buy from the dealer at great cost, or occasionally from the stalls for less than the market value, are indicative of the motive which prompted the purchase, and in a large number of cases this may be summed up in a single phrase—expectancy of gain. Collectors of this type may follow the fashion of the day, or they may bridge over time, and cast their specu-lations like bread upon the waters, in the hope that they may be recompensed hereafter for their present self-denial. The former practice is easy,

and leads to tangible results ; the latter is just
the reverse, for the future decrees of fashion,
though they may be anticipated more or less
successfully, can never be foretold with absolute
precision.

At this moment there are books to be purchased
for trivial sums which will eventually be worth
their weight in gold : this much we know from a
contemplation of the past; but to identify them
among the mass of worthless literature visible on
every hand is a matter of great difficulty, and, to a
large extent, of impossibility.

For anything we know to the contrary, popular
taste may some of these days find itself forced in
the direction of philology, as was the case two
hundred years ago. In this event the Latin or
Greek Grammar which can to-day be bought for a
few pence, may then be worth as many shillings,
or perhaps pounds ; and collectors will sigh for the
good old days, just as they do now when they
allow their thoughts to wander to the beginning of
the century, and see in their mind's eye early
Shakesperian quartos knocked down in dozens
for two or three pounds each. Shakespeare has
now become a name to conjure with, and in the
place of two or three pounds, we must write four
or five hundred, and that with difficulty.

How, then, can we prepare ourselves to take
advantage, not only of present opportunities, but

also of those which may, or at any rate should, occur in the future? There is only one way, that adopted by old Marley's ghost, which reproduced to the vision of Scrooge the events of the past and of the present, which inevitably led, or would have led, to those which were to come.

In journeying round and about the bookstalls nothing must be left to chance. When a book is taken up and thrown aside at the first glance, the reason which prompts the act must be based upon something more than the mere expression, "I do not want it; it is no use to me"—from which it will readily be perceived that it is not to the reader, who has guides enough at his disposal, but to the collector. who has but few, that these remarks mainly apply.

In brief, we must search the past and critically examine the present before it becomes possible to speculate on the future. The ordinary course has been to reverse these processes, and the result has been precisely what might have been expected: the collector has in despair adopted the motto, "Sufficient for the day," and tamely followed the fashion. It remains for a new generation of book-hunters to make the fashion follow them; or, if this cannot be done, through lack of time or means, to come up with it on the instant of its turn. This sounds desirable: the question is, Can it be done? For my part, I feel confident that it

can, and I am confirmed in this belief by the result
of one or two ventures which, though apparently
more than speculative at the time, fell out eventually exactly as I had predicted.

It is well known that, in this country at any
rate, books were, for at least a hundred years or
more after Caxton established his press at West-
minster, both scarce and costly. In 1545 the
library of such a powerful noble as the Earl of
Warwick contained only forty printed books. At
this period a private gentleman of average means,
however many manuscripts he might manage to
collect, was accounted fortunate if his library
numbered a dozen volumes from the press. One
collector, who lived in the early days of Henry
VIII., has catalogued his books on the fly-leaf of
a copy of Cicero, and proudly added up the grand
total. There were copies of Sallust, the Cicero
referred to, Virgil, Xenophon, Alexander, and
Horace, also a Greek Grammar, probably by
Lascaris, a book on logic, and six works of
divinity—fourteen printed books in all. The value
of these would be great ; the task of collecting
them difficult in the extreme.

From this and other evidence it is clear that the
popular taste which then prevailed in the matter
of books was directed mainly towards the classics,
while works of divinity occupied a good second
place. It may possibly be asked why this was the

case, seeing that many other works of a less abstruse nature—Caxton's " Game and Playe of Chesse," and Brandt's " Shyp of Folys," for example—had already been published in England, and were doubtless as easily obtainable in those days as foreign editions of the Epics of Virgil, or Odes of Horace.

The reason is not far to seek. Most manuscripts copied by the monks were either theological or classical in their nature, for laborious writing was not to be employed save on works which were worthy of the necessary sacrifice of time. When printing came into active operation all over the Continent, and to a lesser extent in England, the same considerations prevailed in the main, and classical and theological treatises held almost undisputed sway. The first work ever printed with movable metal types was the Bible, and the printers of the early days would have regarded with disfavour the employment of the press for every trivial, or indeed for any, purpose which they might not consider worthy of the application of the art.

The few people who could read had been trained in a narrow school, and knew their Virgil better than we do now, while a knowledge of theology formed part of their early training. Hence it is not surprising to find that the desire for knowledge was limited to a few, and practi-

cally confined to the graver subjects of interest.
For many years this continued to be the case,
and even during the 17th century, men still
remembered the days of their ancestors and
chose their books accordingly. In 1632 the
house of the Gray Friars at Roane was furnished
with three shelves, fifty-six paces long and one
above the other, upon which were ranged the
2000 volumes of theology and philosophy which
formed the library; while even in 1700 the
collection of books which was presented to the
Grammar School of Leigh, in Lancashire, consisted entirely of the classics and the religious
writings of the Puritan Commonwealth.

The catalogue of Spinoza's books was dis-
covered by the Hague archivist, Servas van
Rooijen. There were 135 volumes in all, con-
sisting of lexicons in various languages, Bibles,
rabbinical works, and medical and mathematical
treatises. The classics comprise the Iliad, Cæsar,
Tacitus, Livy, Sallust, Cicero's Letters, Martial,
Ovid's Metamorphoses, Plautus, the Alexander of
Curtius and Arrianus, Seneca, Pliny's Letters,
Aristotle's Rhetoric, Lucian's Dialogues, Petronius
Arbiter, and Epictetus. Spinoza also possessed
Josephus and an epitome of St. Augustine.

Broadly speaking, it may be asserted that
during the 15th, 16th, and first few years of
the 17th, centuries, and later still in certain

C

instances the book-buyers of this country con-
tented themselves with serious literature. They
bought their books to read, and had plenty of
time on their hands to ponder over them.

The first book auction ever held in England
took place at the house of Dr. Lazarus Seaman,
in Warwick Lane, in 1676; and between that
date and 1682 no less than thirty sales of
books took place in London. The catalogues
of all of them consist almost entirely of the
works of the Fathers and Schoolmen, learned,
critical, and philological works, the writings of
contemporary English and foreign divines of
the Puritan school, and a goodly number of
books and pamphlets, chiefly of the controversial
kind, printed in the reigns of Henry VIII.,
Edward VI., Mary, and Elizabeth. Here and
there appear works in foreign languages giving
accounts of the early voyages to America, which
are now of immense value, but were then thought
so little of as to necessitate several of them being
put together to make one acceptable lot.

In short, books had not then begun to be
multiplied at the same alarming rate as at
present, and many years had yet to elapse before
it would be thought worth anyone's while to write
an oration in praise of mud, or a treatise in
eulogy of an egg or of a glass phial, or even
of a saucepan.

John Norris, the Platonist, used to say that if
the angels used their quills we should have no
more folios, and in those days writers had much
of the angel about them. They wrote comparatively little, but what they did compose was
solid, perhaps a little pedantic, but always
conscientious.

It took a long while for the works of Marlowe
and the succeeding dramatists of the Elizabethan
age to be regarded with favour. They were
doubtless bought and read and then thrown
lightly aside as befitted the character they had
earned. The collector, such as we see him,
hardly existed at all, and no extortionate prices
were ever paid for books : there was in fact as
yet nothing in the nature of bric-à-brac about
them. The modern collector may be said to
have sprung into being during the progress of
the Duke of Roxburghe's sale, which took place
during forty-one days of May and June, 1812.
Never had a collection of 10,000 volumes on
such a diversity of subjects been got together
by an English gentleman before. Theology,
jurisprudence, philosophy, art and science, philology, poetry, the drama, romance, criticism,
geography, history, and antiquarian literature in
most of their branches were all represented,
and attracted a crowd of newly-fledged bookworms who seemingly did not care what they

paid for some of the choicest lots. One MS. on vellum, descriptive of the Arms of the Knights of the Round Table, brought £36 ; Bellenden's "Croniklis of Scotland," £65 ; a copy of the first folio of Shakespeare's complete works, 1623, brought £100, while the Marquis of Blandford broke all previous records and constituted himself the pioneer of the modern book-hunter by writing out a cheque for £2260, that being the figure at which a copy of Valdarfer's Boccaccio of 1471 was knocked down. Caxton's "Recuyell of the Historyes of Troye," 1471, realised £1068 18s., the very same book having sold for £32 11s. at the West Sale, held some forty years before.

In fact, it may be said that the excessive increase in the value of certain kinds of books dates from the sale of this Roxburghe Library and the formation of the Roxburghe Club, in 1812, an increase which has become still further accentuated as the reports of the Sunderland, Syston Park, Crawford, Hardwicke, and other important dispersions which have taken place in our own day, conclusively prove. Before that time, books were cheap so long as they were not new ; and, exceptions apart, rare editions could be picked up on the stalls for ridiculously small sums. They were worth no more, however, for collectors had not yet commenced to work in unison, and seldom found it worth their while to enter into competition. Books were numerous and scholars few, besides which the foreign demand was simply *nil*, and public libraries practically nonexistent. Most of the essentials of competition were therefore absent, and goodly tomes changed hands without a thought of the morrow. The Roxburghe Sale, however, did more than add for the time being to the pecuniary value of a certain class of books. It steadied the market, and for the first time a code of rules was established for the guidance of a new school of collectors. Many of these rules exist to this day, and are acknowledged to be of binding force by those who, as Naudæus would have said, set about "erecting" a library which shall do justice to a refined and educated taste.

During the greater part of the last century collectors of repute were mainly recruited from the ranks of the aristocracy, or perhaps from among country gentlemen with plenty of time on their hands and means at their disposal. Here and there some pale student, whose clothes smelled of the lamp, might deny himself food in order to obtain a coveted volume which for days had been the object of his thoughts, but such instances were rare, and besides by no stretch of imagination could such an enthusiast

be termed a "collector" in the technical accep-
tation of the word. His books were good, but
not magnificent; they were, moreover, bought to
read, and to be gradually thumbed almost out of
recognition; they can be seen now, littering
the stalls—dead, like their owner, and as ragged
as he perhaps was when he parted with them
for the first and last time.

The bookworm of the past was either very
rich or very poor, or else a pedant. In France
it was different, for as early as the year 1700
there were many who denied themselves neces-
saries for the sake of collecting into a library
(where other books were perhaps scarce enough)
as many of those little works from the presses
of the Elzevirs as they could lay their hands
on. They were dying of hunger, some of them,
but their consolation was to be able to say,
"Here are all the poets whom the Elzevirs ever
printed. There are ten examples of each, all
with red letters and all of the right date."
In such a spirit did Richard Heber wander
about the Continent buying up books by the
thousand, and Resbecq purchase the contents
of half-a-dozen booksellers' shops, each of them
for the mere pleasure of turning over a heap
of miscellaneous literature, and perhaps of ex-
tracting an occasional rarity from among the
mass. These men were rich of course, and had the

true mania for accumulation grafted on their souls. They have their humble followers in plenty now, but the school is a new one in this country notwithstanding.

At the beginning of the present century the English book-lover would have thought twice before he tortured his stomach for the mere sake of possessing a book, and moreover the feebleness of competition warranted no such sacrifice. Even the rich bought merely to please themselves, since there were no rules to guide them—no fashionable outlet, in fact, for their money as there is now. They bought anything, and left the ups and downs of the market to those who made their living by its fluctuations. Still they had their likes and dislikes in a mild sort of way, and this fact of course had some influence on the degree of estimation in which particular classes of books were held. In short, the object of the book-buying public was to accumulate a number of good works upon as many subjects as possible, so as to form an all-round library which they flattered themselves they would some day explore. Some of these subjects were more popular than others, and hence a distinction arose which kept the prices down or raised them, as the case might be.

The following tabular analysis will show the

position of the book market about the beginning of the present century :

1. **Theological Works.**—Latin Bibles were not much sought after, even although printed in the 15th century ; English Bibles not much sought after unless of the 16th century. Macklin's edition of 1800 sold well, so did Baskerville's Bible. Greek and French Bibles were in low repute. Theological, or in fact any, works printed by Caxton and De Worde, brought high prices. Biblical commentaries, criticisms, and works of the Fathers sold for very small sums, unless quite recent editions. Polemical works travelled very slowly, original editions of the works of John Knox and one or two other famous divines alone excepted. Volumes of sermons hardly sold at all, and mystical works, like those of Jacob Behmen, went for a shilling or two each. Early Scotch-printed works of this class sold well, the works of the Freethinkers but slowly, being for the most part despised or held in abhorrence.

2. **Works of Jurisprudence.**—These sold very badly unless perfectly new or exceedingly old, so as to rank primarily as specimens of ancient typography. Volumes of reports and statutes, however, sold well.

3. **Social and Political Works.** — Generally speaking, of trivial importance. About this time

a copy of Machiavelli's "Princeps," printed *sine loco* in 1589, sold for 6d. ; the Amsterdam edition of More's "Utopia," 1643, for 1s. 6d., and Hobbes's "Leviathan," London, 1651, for 6d. These seem to have been the prices usually obtained for works of the kind.

4. **Books relating to Parliamentary Procedure and Practice** sold well, Prynne's "Parliamentary Writs," 4 vols., 4to, 1659, &c., frequently bringing as much as £18. The "Journals of the House of Commons," 55 vols., folio, were worth about £14 14s., and the "Journals of the House of Lords," 33 vols., folio, about £8 8s.

5. **Works on Ancient Philosophy.**—These sold well, and, generally speaking, for more than they would do at the present day. The same remark applies to works treating of modern philosophy, morals, &c.

6. **Mathematical Works** of the 17th and 18th centuries, mostly in 4to and folio, sold fairly well.

7. **Works on the Arts and Sciences.**—These covered an immense field. Works containing plates—such, for example, as "The Houghton Gallery"—now came into fashion. Architectural treatises, printed either abroad or in England, and mostly in folio, sound works on natural history like the Paris edition of Buffon's "Histoire Naturelle des Oiseaux," 10 vols., folio, 1771, and

Lewis's "Birds of Great Britain," 7 vols., 4to, 1789, sold very well; but works on agriculture and gardening, with very few exceptions, fell flat. Medical works were hardly sought after at all unless quite new. Works on magic and witchcraft sold fairly well, but good treatises on physiognomy and kindred sciences, like Hunter's translation of Lavater's Essay, 5 vols, 4to, 1789, brought as much or more than they do now.

Poetical Works.—These were mainly classical, and sold well, as classics were then in repute. Some of the early Italian poets, such as Dante, Torquato Tasso, Alamanni, Ariosto, and Aretino, were highly esteemed. French poetry of an early date was, however, in much greater repute, the old Romants especially. Old English poetry or treatises on the poetic art, such as Webbe's "Discourse," London, 1586, and Puttenham's "Arte of English Poesie," 1589, 4to, and in fact all English-printed works of the 16th century on this subject, sold rapidly and well. The quartos of the early part of the 17th century were also much in vogue. Under this head rank Fletcher's "Purple Island," 1633, Rowland's "Diogenes' Lanthorn," Mill's "Night Search," and a vast number of compositions in pamphlet form. Poems which then were modern, like those of Gray, Chatterton, Burns, Ogilvie, Bloomfield, and Southey, were at a very low ebb.

Dramatic Works.—The works of the Eliza-bethan dramatists had recently begun to attract attention, and some of the early Shakespeare quartos brought £2 and £3 apiece, prices which had never been realised for works of the kind before. Bell's "British Theatre," in 34 vols., 1797, once brought more than £20 by auction, and an anonymous play entitled "Patient Grisell," 4to, 1603, no less than £9; but as a rule the plays of Beaumont and Fletcher, Mrs. Aphra Behn, Isaac Bickerstaff, Henry Carey, George Chapman, Colley Cibber, d'Avenant, Dekker, Dibdin, Dryden, Forde, Ben Jonson, Massinger, Shadwell, Shirley, Wycherley, and many other dramatists, could frequently be met with for a shilling or two each, even in the original. Isolated plays like Marlowe's "Dido," 1594, would, however, sometimes sell for as much as £15 or £20: in fact at this time Marlowe's works were much more expensive than those of Shakespeare, the first four folios only excepted. Some of the plays of Middleton and Heywood were also very scarce, £4 and £5 for a small 4to being an ordinary price to pay.

Romances.—All things considered, perhaps old works of romance were at this period the most expensive that could possibly be bought. The chivalries of Amadis de Gaule, Florimont, Guy of Warwick, Huon de Bordeaux, Olivier of Castille, Palmerin of England—all written in French and published at Paris or Rouen during the 16th century, had long been objects of intense interest to many who never thought of forming a library, but were content if they could gather together half-a-dozen of these old romances. During the 16th century, works of this class had poured from the Press in prodigious numbers, and most had probably been torn or otherwise mutilated or altogether destroyed at the advent of the present century. For long years these mendacious narratives had supplied the place of the modern novel. The same remarks apply more or less to the " Decameron" of Boccaccio, the " Novelle " of Bandello, and the " Don Quixote " of Cervantes, and also to other books which crossed the borderline of romance—as, for example, the Legends of King Arthur, of which a considerable number were extant, of Robin Hood, Parismus Prince of Bohemia, the Mythical Knight of the Sea, and the histories of Jack of Newbery and Thomas of Reading. " Robinson Crusoe," " The Castle of Otranto" " The Monk," and Psalmanaazar's " Description of Formosa," all come within this category. Books such as these had formed part of the literature of the people, and old editions in a good state of preservation were consequently scarce.

Works on Philology and Criticism.—These sold well, particularly if comparatively new, like

Walpole's "Anecdotes of Painting," 4 vols., 4to, 1762, or very old. Seventeenth century editions were, however, for the most part in ill repute, as also were those of the sixteenth, unless printed in England.

Satirical and Amusing Works were in high estimation, whether classical, like the "Golden Ass" of Apuleius; mediæval, like the works of Rabelais; or modern. Original editions of Robert Greene's black-letter quartos sold for several guineas each.

Fables and Emblems sold fairly well, the most in favour being old editions of Æsop and Holbein's "Dance of Death."

Tracts.—These occupied a curious position, and their importance depended entirely on their subject-matter. Theological tracts were nearly all worthless, so were most of those in foreign languages, classical or otherwise. Many tracts printed in England during the Elizabethan age were, however, scarce, as also were some of those published in such numbers during the time of the Civil Wars. Anything that could be classed under "Drama" or "Romance," or in some cases "Poetry," received attention.

Geographical Works were in good repute if they contained old maps. Blaeu's "Atlas Major," in 12 vols., folio, 1662, for example, was worth

£8 or £10, and Saxton's "Atlas" almost as much. In any other event new works were better than old.

Voyages and Travels.—Modern treatises, like Cook's "Voyages" sold for large sums, but the older books appear to have been regarded as out of date, and consequently of but little value. English-printed 16th century books were, however, as usual, competed for at good prices. The few 15th century books of this class in the market, *e.g.*, Breydenbach's Voyage, folio, Lyons, 1488, brought most of all, doubtless as curiosities.

Works on Ancient History, Jewish, Greek, or Norman, were but little sought after, unless 15th or 18th century editions, when they sold well, the latter especially. Gibbon's "Decline and Fall," in 6 vols., 4to, 1776-81, was worth more, for example, than many of the 15th century editions of Sallust or Tacitus.

Works on Ecclesiastical History were thought little of, and sold, as a rule, for small sums.

Works on Continental History were generally arranged in large libraries, under the countries to which they related. Many of the more modern ones were regarded with great interest.

Works on English History.—Upon the principle that it is disgraceful to know nothing of the history of the country to which one belongs, it was the ambition of all large collectors to show as varied an assortment under this head as possible, and prices in the main were excessively high. Topographical works were included under this heading, and prices which were often paid for these would now be considered absurd. Dugdale's "Monasticon" of 1655, for example, would sell for £50 or more, and the same author's "Historie of Imbanking and Drayning," 1662, for nearly £20 if well bound and in good condition.

Works relating to America.—Many of these were getting rare and sold for tolerable sums. Modern works were, however, still in greater request than old ones.

Antiquarian Works, if modern, were much sought after, particularly if in folio with large plates. Works on architecture and gems, in folio, had a good sale.

Biographical Works, unless of recent date, travelled slowly. An exception occurred, as usual, in favour of 15th century works—such, for example, as the *editio princeps* of Cornelius Nepos, Venice, 1471, which about this time was worth £7 or £8.

Such was the position of the English book market at the commencement of the present century. Henceforth collectors vied with each other to procure works which had been authoritatively regarded with approval, and libraries were built up to a very large extent on the Roxburghe catalogue alone. The institution of the Roxburghe Society also acted as a stimulant to the book-collector, and testified to the growing interest in many ancient tracts and works of general interest which the Society was founded to reprint.

Several generations of collectors have lived and died since these early days, and the present century has witnessed a partial revolution in the tastes and desires of their successors. Even now, however, the state of the market can be directly traced to the influences which were at work eighty years and more ago, and any competent person who had then thought it worth his while to prophesy what would happen in our day should have been able to do so successfully from the evidence before him. We have more details at our disposal than our forefathers ever had, and there can be little doubt that the record of twenty years to come is already staring us in the face if we choose to look at it for the benefit either of ourselves or of those who are destined to take our place.

The popular taste of to-day has grown by degrees. It is, moreover, evolved, not created. The popular taste of the next century will be the outcome and natural result of that which prevails now. It is necessary, therefore, to study the present, and to draw a comparison between it and the past. This proposition has been laid down previously, and the reasons in support of it will be sufficiently apparent from what has already been said.

CHAPTER III.

THE MODERN BOOK-HUNTER.

OF late years the number of illustrated books has increased with marvellous rapidity. The Bewicks were the first to rescue the art of engraving from the degraded position into which it had fallen in this country, and no sooner was their genius recognised than collectors began to look around for any works which might contain their woodcuts. Thomas Bewick, the more talented artist of the two, adopted a method of exciting the cupidity of his admirers by publishing his works in limited editions and on paper of various sizes, and of course at various prices. This system stimulated the sale and amounted to a practical recognition of the collector as a being distinct from the ordinary man of letters. From the days of Bewick until now, collectors have been eager to secure illustrated works which for any reason would be likely to increase in

value as time went on, and it is only fair to
say that authors and publishers have done their
best to keep pace with the demand.

Putting aside the visionary William Blake,
who worked from conscientious motives, and
Bartolozzi, who will be referred to subsequently,
we recognise in Rowlandson, the apostle of
the new cult—a partner, in fact, with William
Combe and a number of other literary hacks,
whose sole object it was to minister to a taste
which a few years before would have been looked
upon as depraved, but which nevertheless was
all but universal at the time. The "Pleasures
of Human Life," by "Hilaris Benevolus and Co.,"
"Advice to Sportsmen," by "Marmaduke Mark-
well, Esq.," "Adventures of Qui Hi in Hindostan,"
and a number of other publications of a similar
kind, the titles of which proclaim their frivolous
nature, took the place of sober treatises, and
educated the public for the advent of Pierce
Egan and his school, who went still further in
the same direction. These books were bought
with avidity, partly on account of the lightness
of the text, which afforded an agreeable relief to
the style which had hitherto been prevalent, but
chiefly for the sake of the illustrations, more often
than not coloured by hand, and always grotesque
or bizarre.

The revival of pugilism—originating, in the

opinion of a learned divine of the age, "in a
ferocious disposition and a contemptuous opinion
of man"—and the prevalence of such sports as
bear-baiting, badger-drawing, and cock-fighting,
afforded a rare field of enterprise, and during the
first quarter of the present century numerous
works with coloured plates were published for the
amusement of those who took a delight in pas-
times of the kind. "Life in London" and "Life
in Paris" furnish good examples of the kind of
literature which was in circulation about the year
1820, and which afforded ample scope for the
rising genius of Cruikshank.

Some ten or a dozen years after the completion
of the second decade a visible reaction set in,
and drawing-room tables all over the country were
soon littered with a new phase of art. At this
epoch fine steel-plates became the fashion, and
many excellent artists, such as Finden, Harding,
and Prout, contributed, though not for long, to
exalt the popular taste.

The public, however, soon got tired of Fisher's
"Drawing Room Scrap Book," and the host of
elegant miscellanies which were served up for
their delectation, and returned to their old love
under the guidance of Cruikshank and Leech,
Ohwhyn, "Phiz," Seymour, Alken, Doyle, and
other artists of the same racy school. Not that
all these artists can fairly be classed either to-

gether or with Rowlandson and his followers; on the contrary, they differed widely both in style and excellence, and the intervening period of moral depression had unmistakably qualified the tendency to vulgarity which had been so conspicuous in the earlier part of the century.

Of all the books sought after by the collector of average means, the productions of the old sporting, gambling school yet remain pre-eminent, or at any rate rank equally with those illustrated by Cruikshank, "Phiz," and the other masters whose merit lies not so much in fidelity to nature as in the strangeness of their compositions. All these books, and many more of the same class, passed through many hands before they became scarce; and the contrast between the value of a clean and sound copy and one which bears the thumb-marks of a generation of readers, is often exceedingly wide. Still, whether dirty or tattered or the reverse, perfect or imperfect, in the original binding or in the best style of Rivière or Bedford, these books never fail to sell at a price which seems to be increasing every day.

This result might indeed have been anticipated a hundred years ago, for at that time, or a little later, the plates of Bartolozzi, Gillray, and Rowlandson, though widely different in every respect, clearly pointed to the success which would be attained by any future artist who should be so fortunate as to fall in with the popular taste. Rowlandson is the connecting link between the past and the present in one respect at least ; he set a fashion which has only ceased to attract because there is no one capable of filling his place. The book-hunter, however, has plenty of scope, and no works are so eagerly sought after at the present time as those which are illustrated by one or other of the artists I have named. It must be distinctly understood that reference is not made to " Art Books," popularly so called, as these, with but few exceptions, among which the works of Ruskin and Hamerton stand almost alone, have been distinctly deteriorating in value of late years. Whether they will ever recover their former position is a question for the next chapter rather than for this.

The Roxburghe Sale taught many lessons. One we have learned, the others have mainly to do with that class of works which relate to the American continent and were printed during the 16th and 17th centuries, specimens of old typography from early English presses, works printed in Scotland at any time previous to the year 1715, or within a few years after that date, early editions of old English authors, works on natural history with coloured plates, English Bibles of the 16th century, old romances, antiquarian folios with large plates, topographical works of the better class, and ancient English or Scotch poetry. At the beginning of the century, books which answered any of these descriptions were rising in value every day; and it was therefore only fair to assume that others of a like nature, though perhaps not exactly similar, would do the same.

When people begin to collect articles of any kind it is always found that the scope of their operations eventually becomes too limited, and other articles similar in their nature are in process of time classed with the rest. Hence, when we know that at a certain date English Bibles of the 16th century were in request, it is easy to see that it was merely a question of time for those of the 17th century to be regarded with favour also. At the time of the Roxburghe Sale such Bibles were of very little value, and might be bought for as many shillings—or less— as they often now cost pounds. There would have been no magic in this prophecy. The newest books grow old at last: the touch of time may sober their bravery, prices may increase or decrease, readers may change, but the future of the bookworm always lies in the same direction.

All classes of books which were rising in value at the time of the Roxburghe Sale—which we have taken as being, on the whole, the most satisfactory dispersion for our purpose—are, with a solitary exception, sought after now. Others which were then in ill repute are, without any exception, in ill repute now. Theological works of the more ponderous kind, such as commentaries and criticisms, which were all very well in a Puritan or bigoted age ; volumes of sermons delivered with much pomposity and show of erudition, like those of Donne, who interlarded every other sentence with a Latin or Greek quotation ; 17th century works on philology and criticism, geographical works too old to be of any practical use but not old enough to be regarded as curiosities, historical and biographical works of a similar nature : all these, which at one time were read and re-read by the studious, had fallen upon evil days and came to be sold for a song. Would they ever recover their position again? a bookworm of eighty years ago might have asked, and had he done so his instinct would have supplied the answer. When education should be limited to the few, and narrow controversy come to usurp the place of religion, then would such works once again stand pre-eminent over all others.

The solitary exception alluded to consists of classical works, which were in 1812 largely purchased, possibly by many who would have found considerable difficulty in reading them.

At that time such works sold well, and in

fact they continued to increase in value until some thirty or forty years ago, when they suddenly, and apparently without any reason, lost favour, and have continued to fall in the market ever since. Reference is not made to editions which rank as curiosities, such as the Virgil printed by Sueynheym and Pannartz at Rome in 1469, for a copy of which an enthusiastic collector recently paid no less than £590; but to scholarly editions like those of Hearne, Bryan, Bekker, Heyne, and other learned editors of the 18th century. It is these which have fallen so low of late years, to such an extent indeed that no modern edition of any classical author whatever has maintained its former reputation from a pecuniary point of view. Even the masterly productions of Aldus Manutius are esteemed no longer by any but the student, while the reprints of the Elzevirs have long since ceased to be regarded with the enthusiasm of Charles Nodier, who left a space which he declared should never be profaned by any Virgil but the little Leyden edition of 1636 with its passages in red and textual errors on every page. Fifty years ago a "tall" copy of this "right" Elzevir Cæsar would have sold for £70 or more. In 1878 such a copy actually brought £50; the other day these prices had fallen to £2 10s. In England, as in France, it was, and indeed is, customary to measure these little books to the twenty-fifth part of an inch, and the "taller" a copy the more it is likely to be worth ; but I think I am justified in saying that there is no copy of the Cæsar of 1636 existing on the earth at the present moment, however fair and however "tall," which would bring a sum of £70 at auction, or anything approaching that amount.

It may indeed be taken for granted that unless an edition of a Greek or Latin classic is from such a noted press as to rank primarily as a rare and important specimen of ancient typography, it is, as a rule, of very little value. The text may be accurate, infinite pains may have been taken to secure the most authentic readings, words and sentences may have been studied and pronounced of doubtful authenticity or the reverse, in elaborate notes indicative of the profoundest learning,— everything, in fact, may have been done to insure perfection as far as that quality is capable of being attained, but all to no purpose from a pecuniary point of view.

The classics indeed are out of date, and for the simple reason that scholars are rare. At the beginning of the century the case was otherwise ; the spirit which prompted the purchase of solid works was not yet quite extinct. The cumbrous theological folios had indeed fallen into obscurity, but the classics were admired, not only by thousands who took a genuine pleasure in reading them, but by many others who sought to acquire a reputation for learning, and thought that the accumulation of a number of grave and learned books was the easiest way of attaining their end. That the pecuniary value of such books should have increased for a time is not so surprising as that it should now have fallen to almost zero.

This is a genuine example of the vagaries of fashion, to which even the staid book-collector is subject with the rest of mankind.

Classical works are not fashionable now: of that there cannot be the shadow of a doubt. Lighter literature has usurped the position formerly held by the poets and historians of Greece and Rome, and it is fortunate for us that it is so, for we hold in our hands the shadowy link between the present and the future. One of the most powerful facts which it is possible to adduce in evidence as a guide to the future state of the book-market, lies in this apparent neglect of a time-honoured literature. Can it continue? Time alone will show. In the next chapter I hope to bridge over the intervening period in this and other respects, and the bookworm of the future will know whether the prophecy is warranted by the result.

It may be useful at this stage to call attention

to various special works of reference which are commonly consulted by modern collectors.

For Anonymous and Pseudonymous Literature—Halkett and Laing's "Dictionary," 4 vols., impl. 8vo, 1882-88.

For Collectors of Works from the Elzevir Press — Willems' "Les Elzevier, Histoire et Annales Typographiques," Brussels, 8vo, 1880; Goldsmid's "Bibliotheca Curiosa," 8vo, 1889 (a valuable work in this series for those who do not read French).

For Collectors of Works from the Aldine Press — Renouard's "Annales de l'imprimerie des Alde," Paris, 3 vols., 8vo, 1825.

For Black-letter Collectors — Ames' "Typographical Antiquities," with additions by Herbert and Dibdin, 4 vols., 4to, 1810-19; the British Museum "Catalogue of Early-Printed Books in English," carried down to the year 1640; Maitland's "Early-Printed Books in the Lambeth Library," carried down to 1600.

For Collectors of Privately-Printed Works—Martin's "Privately-Printed Books," 2nd ed., 8vo, 1854.

For Collectors of Broadsides—Lemon's "Catalogue of Broadsides in the Possession of the Society of Antiquaries," 8vo, 1866.

For Collectors of American Works—Stevens' "Catalogue of American Books in the Library of the British Museum," 8vo, 1866.

For Collectors of Bibles—Dore's "Old Bibles," 8vo, 1889.

For Collectors of Greek and Latin Classics—Dibdin's. "Rare and Valuable Editions of the Greek and Latin Classics," 2 vols., 1827.

For Collectors of Works on Occult Philosophy—Scribner's "Bibliotheca Diabolica," New York, 4to, 1874; also the catalogues issued by George Redway (Trübner and Co., Ludgate Hill).

For Dickens Collectors — C. P. Johnson's "Hints to Collectors of Original Editions of Dickens' Works," 8vo, 1885.

For Thackeray Collectors — C. P. Johnson's "Hints to Collectors of Original Editions of the Works of W. M. Thackeray," 8vo, 1885. The same author's "Early Writings of William M. Thackeray," 8vo, 1888.

For Cruikshank Collectors — G. W. Reid's "Descriptive Catalogue of the Works of George Cruikshank," London, 8vo, 1871.

For Collectors of the Works of Carlyle, Swinburne, Ruskin, and Tennyson — R. H. Shepherd's catalogues of the works of each of these authors. See also the "Ruskin Bibliography" (Richard Clay and Sons).

For Collectors of the Works of Hazlitt, Leigh Hunt, and Lamb — Alexander Ireland's catalogues of the works of each of these authors.

For Bewick Collectors—Hugo's "Bewick Collector," 2 vols., 8vo, 1866-68.*

---

* *This list is extracted from my* "Library Manual," 3rd edition, 1891 (L. Upcott Gill, 170, Strand, W.C.).

CHAPTER IV.

TEN YEARS HENCE OR LESS.

THE same reasons which forced a book up in the market about the time of the Roxburghe Sale, and have continued to exalt or debase it, from a pecuniary point of view, during the period between then and now, are useful for the purpose of ascertaining what the popular taste of the future should be. Several of these reasons are explained in the previous chapters, and the book-hunters of the 20th century will be as much bound by them as our progenitors were, and as we are bound to-day.

Most people look upon fashion, even in book-collecting, as the outcome of mere chance, but it is founded rather on well-defined rules, not one of which can be broken with impunity. The times change certainly, and we change with them, but not suddenly. On the contrary, what we call change is either advancement or retrogression along the same beaten track.

When someone acts contrary to the ordinary usages of society he is called eccentric, and if very eccentric, mad; and though I doubt not there are many who would be prepared to follow a great personage, no matter to what height of eccentricity he might soar, the fashion thus set would be a fashion only in name, and as unstable as extraordinary and irrational.

The book-hunter is in one respect in a much more favourable position than the mere follower of a fleeting custom, for he has the records of many past years to guide his course of action. Should he desire to establish a rule of his own making however, it is almost certain that others would regard his example with indifference.

There is a reason even for this, and it lies in the fact that a man who collects books is offended if it is suggested that he does not, or, worse still, cannot read and understand them, and as he actually or nominally buys his books to read, he is prepared to resent any interference with regard to his method of spending his time among them. Suggestions and advice are also thrown away, for although the name of a new or particularly good book is often received with thanks, no one likes to have a course of reading mapped out for him.

The collector's reason for his choice is always dominated by his own likes and dislikes, and he chooses, in the vast majority of cases, to move along the beaten track, simply because he sees others traversing the same course. When fifty or a hundred people simultaneously rush in the same direction, the motive which actuates them is founded upon a reason of some kind, and is not the outcome of chance.

The position taken up, therefore, is that no man however exalted can set a fashion in book-collecting, unless he has good excuses for his choice, and unless also the just grounds of his conclusions are obvious to others at a glance. It is useless trying to support a fashion by argument, for this would be to pre-suppose a doubt. The reason must be patent, or it is worthless.

In this chapter we hold in our mind's eye the collector of the future, and endeavour to point in the direction towards which his inclinations should turn. Then, as now, he will be guided by the popular movement, for which he may have no explanation to offer, but which, nevertheless, is certain to proceed according to rules, well or ill-defined. These must be analysed, and if the operation is skilfully conducted the result should be relieved of much of the uncertainty which has hitherto surrounded every movement of the book market.

E

1. Books of a racy description, with coloured plates by such artists as Rowlandson and Alken, are, as we have seen, tolerably scarce, particularly when in good condition. They comprise facetiæ, sporting books, and works more or less fantastical. Some of them are prurient, others are vulgar to our taste, but every one commands a ready sale at prices which cannot fail to increase as time goes on. Similarly, books illustrated by the later school of artists, which includes the Cruikshanks, Hablot Browne ("Phiz"), Seymour, Leech, and some others, are also a good investment, if in sound condition, but not otherwise. Most of the original editions of Dickens, Thackeray, Ainsworth, Surtees, and Lever come within this category, but there is not the same demand for second editions, and I do not think much will be made out of them for many years to come. A second edition in fine condition is, however, preferable to a dirty or mutilated original, a point worth bearing in mind by those who buy inferior copies because they are cheap. The plates in some of the works of this class are occasionally coloured by hand ; some copies on the contrary are found with the plates uncoloured. A familiar example of this dual state is afforded by Cruikshank's "Loving Ballad of Lord Bateman," 1851. When coloured the value is considerably higher than it otherwise would be.

One word may be added on the desirability of purchasing imperfect copies. If these can be procured at a greatly reduced price, they might be accepted, but not if the edges of the leaves have been cut down by the binder. Such works are dear at any price, and will never be of any greater importance than they are now.

The leaves, and particulary the plates, should be counted, and if time permits, the book collated with some other copy known to be in sound and perfect condition, for the loss of a plate will frequently reduce the value of a book by as much as twenty-five or thirty per cent.

If a collector is asked why he accumulates works of the description referred to, he will generally reply that it is because the authors enjoy a high reputation, and the original editions of their works being produced under their own superintendence are much more likely to be textually accurate than ones which were not so closely scrutinised. This reason is so far satisfactory that it must at last universally prevail, though there can be very little doubt that the illustrations are really the main attraction in almost all cases of the kind.

2. If, therefore, we search for original editions which are not illustrated, but which can be brought within the reason mentioned, we must be on the right track. It must, however, be understood that

the pecuniary value of an original copy of any author's work is in exact proportion to the degree of estimation in which his genius is held, not at the time when he lived, nor at any intervening period, but *now*. Hence we see the early quartos of Shakespeare selling for enormous sums, though there is not a woodcut in any of them. Original editions of Scott's single works, which might be expected to bring a fair price, according to this rule, do not sell for more than a few shillings each. Byron is almost in the same condition, Shelley is better, but still at a comparatively low ebb. All these works, and many more, were produced under the respective authors own eyes, and yet they are of trivial account. How is this? Simply because the rule is yet undeveloped to its full extent. I feel persuaded that any book-hunter who will take the trouble to purchase originals of Scott, Byron, or Shelley, and to keep them free from dirt and damp, will reap a rich harvest before long.

A little while ago, first editions of Tennyson's "Maud," 1855, "Idylls of the King," 1859, "Enoch Arden," 1864, "The Holy Grail," 1870, "Gareth and Lynette," 1872, and "Harold," 1877, sold by auction for less than £1 each, and this, notwithstanding the fact that they were all uncut and uniformly bound by Rivière at considerable expense. These books, too, should be worth five or six times as much as they are now in the near future, and the same remark applies to the works of Browning, and, in fact, to those of every poet who rises above the common level.

These remarks have reference to single pieces only, and not to "complete editions," which, unless of a respectable antiquity, or the best in the market, have no upward tendency, but rather the reverse.

3. All books illustrated by the Bewicks, especially those on large paper, should increase in value, but such increase will be slow. In addition to the " Quadrupeds," " Birds," and " Fables," Thomas Bewick illlustrated a considerable number of minor volumes, such as the Poetical Works of Burns, Alnwick, 1808, Way's Translation of "Le Grand Fabliaux," 1796-1800, Gay's " Fables," Newcastle, 1779, the Letters of "Junius," 2 vols., 8vo., 1797, and Somerville's "Chase," 1796, 4to. Books of this kind have every prospect of rising proportionately higher in the market than the more important productions of the same master.

4. An "Art Book" is one which depends for its reputation upon the quality of its plates, combined sometimes, though not always, with excellence in the text. As a rule, there has been a great fall in the value of books of this kind. All Ruskin's and Hamerton's works, however, are sure to increase in value, and so are those containing

plates of first-rate quality by or after Hogarth, Turner, or Stothard, as for example the 1830 edition of Rogers's "Italy," and the 1834 edition of the same author's "Poems." As a rule, these "Art Books" are dangerous in the extreme, and it is no uncommon circumstance to find a work which was originally published at £40 or £50 sold at auction for a tenth part of the money. In my opinion, all works purely artistic will either deteriorate in value for many years to come or else remain at the same dead level at which they now are. What are known as "Galleries," that is, works containing engravings of noted picture collections, should especially be avoided. There is no prospect of any bargain in them, but rather the reverse.

5. Works relating to the American continent, and printed either in England or in any European country during the 16th and 17th centuries, have recently made extraordinary strides in public favour Many years ago, indications of an upward tendency were clearly discernible, though perhaps no one ever suspected that the rarest of such books would realise the enormous sums which are occasionally paid for them. At the sale of the Wimpole Library, in June 1888, nine small tracts bound in a single volume, realised £66, and another lot of twelve tracts, no less a sum than £555. These pieces were, of course, so excessively

rare that it is hardly worth while speculating on
their future in the market. It is safe to assume,
however, that none would ever be allowed to pass
either now or hereafter without strong competition. Many works of this class, however, are not
so hopelessly out of the reach of the private collector, and there is, moreover, a very fair chance
of an accidental "find," for they mostly look
mean, and are not infrequently small in bulk.
They should never be put aside if they can be got
for a reasonable price, as they are certain to
increase in value. All books printed in the States
during the 18th century are in the same position
and a similar remark applies to any works printed
in Scotland at any time previous to the year 1715.
Irish printed books are not of the same importance,
and it is not worth the while of any but a very
few to collect those in the vernacular. These are
few in number and rare.

6. Of late years a large trade has sprung up
with the colonies, and books descriptive of any
country find a good and ready sale in that to
which they refer. Thus Gage's "Survey of the
West Indies," 1648, folio, worth here some 25s.
or 30s. by auction, would sell for more at Kingston
Jamaica. Books relating to Australia or New
Zealand would also sell well at Melbourne,
Sydney, or Wellington, and the same is true of
other colonies possessing a rapidly increasing

population and a literature of their own. As a consequence, books of this character are bought up to be exported, and of their ultimate rarity in this country there can be little doubt. Books of African travel, about which there was recently so much talk, are in precisely the same position, only in this case the market is not yet developed. It must be understood that reference is not made to newly published works, but only to those which are out of print. The former usually fall considerably in the market immediately after publication, and it takes many years for the value of a second-hand copy to equal the published price, and longer still to exceed it. Books of this class should seldom be bought new, and very rarely subscribed for. Occasionally a book published by subscription will justify the expectations so lavishly raised in the prospectus, but not often. The rule is to buy second-hand a month or two after publication. For one increased amount that will have to be paid, there will probably be ninety-nine instances in which 50 per cent. or more on the published price will be saved.

7. Early editions of old English authors, whether prose or poetry, have always been great favourites with collectors. Many libraries, indeed, hardly consist of anything else, and as the records of the past disclose a steady upward tendency, and as, moreover, this is just the class of literature

which an educated man is likely to wish to have at his fingers' ends, old books of the kind are not only certain to keep their position in the future but to become more valuable as time goes on. It is not every book, however, even of this description which is valuable or likely to become so. On the contrary, some are quite worthless, and great care has to be exercised in their selection. Then there are certain rules which all collectors follow, and as these ought to be well known, even if they are not, it becomes necessary to run through them, even at the risk of being considered prosaic or hypercritical.

Of all the old English-printed books the most valuable are those which rank primarily as specimens of ancient typography, indeed, it is no exaggeration to say that these are not as a rule within the reach of the ordinary collector at all. They are either bought, on the rare occasions on which they occur for sale, by the owners of large private libraries to whom the expenditure of a score of pounds more or less is a matter of no moment, or else they become buried in the public institutions of this country or abroad.

The latter destination is the more probable, and inasmuch as there is no instance on record of the voluntary dispersion of a public library, it is safe to assume that a book once within the walls of such an institution is practically buried for ever. For this reason, among others, the works of Caxton and other early English printers of the 15th century are not to be got except by the merest accident, and then only at an exorbitant price.

Occasionally, indeed, news of a discovery more or less authentic finds its way into the columns of the press, but the occurrence is so rare as to amount to nothing more than a nine days wonder. The details of some of these "finds" are very amusing, and not infrequently reflect rather unfavourably on the common sense of those who participate in them. For instance, one of the half-dozen perfect or imperfect copies of the "Book of St. Albans," printed by an unknown typographer in 1486, was sold to a pedlar for 9d. when the library at Thorneck Hall was weeded of its superfluous volumes. The pedlar sold it to a chemist at Gainsborough for 3s., who in his turn handed it to a bookseller for £2. He made £5 by re-selling it to another bookseller, who eventually sold it to Sir Thomas Grenville for £80, and at his death it found its way with the rest of his books to the British Museum, where it can be seen at any time gorgeously bound, and no longer a subject of speculation. All this took place notwithstanding the fact that a very imperfect copy had sold many years before for £147, and that Dibdin assessed a perfect specimen at £420. At the present time the value must be close on double that amount, for in 1882 Messrs. Christie, Manson, and Woods disposed of a copy by auction for 600 guineas.

These specimens of early typography, whether English or foreign printed, disclose their character on their very face. The quaintness of the type, the rudeness of the woodcuts, if there are any, and the general *tout ensemble* are sufficient in themselves to put the most ignorant vendor on his guard. It is consequently an accident of an accident for such a book to find its way into the market at anything less than its value, while the occasion of its appearance is rare in the extreme. A single leaf of any of Caxton's works is worth £1 as a curiosity, and, in fact, all his books and those of many other printers anterior and subsequent to him are nothing but curiosities.

I think, therefore, we may leave all 15th century books (though many of those printed abroad are not of much pecuniary value) with the remark that there are no bargains to be made out of them, since the possessor is more apt to overvalue than to undervalue any example he may have.

Books of the 16th century are, however, legitimate objects of search, and with regard to these great discrimination has to be used. If printed abroad they may be of value, though the chance is against their being so; if printed in England the rule is precisely the reverse, and so far as works of this description and date are concerned it is better never to pass one by without being quite certain that the price asked is too high.

As English-printed books of the 15th century are exceedingly scarce and valuable, so these 16th-century books will some day be worth far more than they are now. Time is slipping along, and their numbers are decreasing yearly. Buy, therefore, whenever possible, always remembering the probability that the price asked will be either as much as or more than it should be, or else considerably less. The sum demanded is really of very great importance, for we may be very well certain that no one would ask as much as £1 for a book unless he had satisfied himself as to its actual worth. If he asks pence the chances are at least even that his knowledge is limited or non-existent.

Book-hunters who beguile their leisure moments in searching costermongers' barrows and diving down pestilential courts and alleys in the hope of snapping up some unconsidered trifle in the shape of an *editio princeps* are but mortal after all. They sometimes drive hard bargains, and are not infrequently strangers to the truth in their dealings with those whose want of knowledge would make them a still easier prey were it not for that strange psychological influence which tells them they are being imposed upon. When one of the fraternity takes from its shelf a remarkably fine copy of a rare book, for which he informs you in a stage whisper he gave sixpence, he frequently omits to mention several other little items which ought to be brought into the account, and which Chatterton would have made out in his own peculiar and very original way. It seems as though the scarcest book is sometimes paid for too dearly, and when this is the case it is usually because it has cost not the most but the least.

Foreign-printed books of the 16th century are, comparatively speaking, common, and five out of six are worthless. Theological and philosophical treatises and classical works, particularly those in Greek characters, are very rarely of value, and the same remark applies to the Latin works of the grammarians, as well as to medical and law books. These comprise a no inconsiderable portion of the contents of the bookstalls in this country as well as abroad. The books of this class, which are valuable and likely to increase in value as time goes on, include the French romances, travels in any language, poetry in any language, historical works in any language except Latin and Greek, for many of these consist of bad editions of the classics, than which there are none worse than the majority of those

published during the 16th century. Books printed
by Aldus Manutius, at Venice, though scholarly,
have of late years much deteriorated in value,
as already explained. It would be advisable to
buy any of these (which cannot be dated earlier
than 1495, nor later than 1515), as in my opinion
they are certain to regain their former position
in the market before many years have elapsed.
Already there are signs of an increased interest
in the classics, and those printed by Aldus
Manutius are the best of their kind, even
in these days of school editions. This branch
of the subject is referred to more fully later
on.

From what has been said the book-hunter
will have learned to keep a sharp look-out for
15th and 16th century books, particularly those
printed in England. My practice has latterly
been to buy any book answering this description,
even although I know nothing about it; for even
if it should turn out to be worthless the experi-
ment is worth trying—assuming, of course, that
the work can be got for a small sum. No one
can possibly tell the value of every work he
sees—many indeed he may never have heard
of in his life before; and when this is the case
all he can do is to exercise his judgment.
This he does by assigning the book which puzzles
him to a particular class and comparing it

with others of the same class which he knows
to be of value or the reverse.

During the reigns of Elizabeth, James I., and the
two Charles's the English press was busily occupied in the production of a good deal of light and
ephemeral literature—if indeed the works of the
poets and dramatists merit the former appellation
as those of the pamphleteers certainly deserve the
latter. Many of these are of the highest degree
of rarity, and here again the primary rule to be
followed is based upon the maxim already
elaborated. As is the genius of an author, so is
the pecuniary value of the original editions of
his works. As that genius is highly or lightly
esteemed at different periods of time, so does
the value of his works rise or fall in the market.
It must be understood, however, that in the vast
majority of cases it is only original editions
which are of value—unless indeed the reputation of the author is sufficiently high to carry
the value on, so to speak, to a second or subsequent edition. This rule holds good all but
universally, except that in more recent times
a second or subsequent edition may be worth
more than the first, by reason of its containing
for the first time illustrations by some artist of
repute. I am not speaking now of collected
works published in a number of volumes, but
of single pieces as they were published by the

author—as, for example, Robin Greene's "Fare-well to Follie," 1617, or Thomas Heywood's "Silver Age," 1613, both in small 4to.

Also let it remembered that a book to be of value for its text alone must have been published during the lifetime of the author. If published after his death, any value it may possess will depend upon other considerations, as is the case with Halliwell's edition of Shakespeare's works, 16 vols., 1853-65, a copy of which recently sold by auction for over £70. Here it was not the reputation of Shakespeare so much as that of his great critic, Mr. Halliwell-Phillipps, which caused the book to sell so well. So far as the works of Shakespeare are concerned, a marvellously correct modern edition can be got for a shilling.

When a book-hunter happens to come across a single piece (never mind collected works unless almost contemporary with the author), particularly if in small quarto, let him consider whether the edition is original or not. Most likely he will be unable to remember, but at any rate he can guess to within a few years. If the price asked is small, the book should be bought at a venture, particularly when the author is a celebrity in the world of letters, for in this case his name will impress a value on many editions subsequent to the first. Thus, any edition of the quartos of Shakespeare are valuable, though the reader is hardly likely to be troubled with a superfluity of these.

This reminds me to mention an important fact connected with the great dramatist. Not only are early editions of his own works valuable, but also those editions of other works which he consulted during the compilation of his inimitable plays. It is well known that Shakespeare borrowed many of his plots from the works of other authors, who thus absorb no little of his reflected glory. "Shakespeare's Library," as it is called, which contains a collection of the romances, novels, poems, and histories used by Shakespeare as the foundation of his dramas, was edited by J. P. Collier, and published in 1843 in 2 vols., 8vo.

From the foregoing remarks the works of Milton, even when in the original, must to a large extent be excluded. The "Paradise Lost," for example, was first published in 1667-9, and a good copy of this edition is of no greater value than about £15. Some of his other works, such as "Lycidas," 1638, are, however, worth four or five times this amount, though even that, as prices go, is not a very large sum to pay when the rule as to personal reputation is taken into consideration. The reason of the exception is that Milton's works, particularly those of later date, were published in large quantities; they appealed also to a very different class of readers than did those of the dramatists. Shakespeare's early quartos must have been destroyed in hundreds by the reckless frequenters of " The Globe," when the staid and sober Puritans of Milton's age were yet unborn.

One other rule has to be noted before we leave the old English author and his productions. This is, never to pass a volume of poetry in English dated before 1700. Many, or indeed most, of these are particularly scarce and valuable. The names of the poets who flourished during the 18th century are known to nearly all, but not so those of the previous century. It might be easy to pass by the " Purple Island" of Phineas Fletcher or the " Lucasta " of the courtly Lovelace, but not if this latter rule is kept continually before the mind's eye.

8. For many years it has been the custom to collect editions and versions of the Old and New Testaments, either in Latin or English, or both. Some of the Latin Bibles are very old, dating as far back as the 15th century, but curiously enough they are not particularly valuable. The vast majority bring no more than £2 or £3 by auction ; many produce even less. Of course there are exceptions, such as the famous Mazarin Bible, the first book printed with movable metal types, a copy of which sold at the Syston Park

sale for no less than £3900. As a rule, however, these old Latin Bibles are not worth much, and they can certainly never be bought for much less than their value. Their antiquity betrays them at the first glance, and, as in many other cases, the owner is nearly always under the impression that he has a small fortune within his grasp. The value put upon these books by non-professional owners is usually greatly in excess of their real worth.

English-printed Bibles are, however, in quite a different position. Some are of very great rarity, particularly when perfect and in the original bindings. As a rule, the original edition of each version is the most important, and the older the work the more valuable it is likely to be. The first English Bible is known as "Coverdale's Bible," and was printed in 1535; the latest in date which interests collectors is dated 1717, and is known as the "Vinegar Bible" from the heading to the twentieth chapter of Luke, which reads, "The Parable of the Vinegar." The numerous, and for the most part cumbrous Bibles issued after 1717 are well-nigh worthless, and this although many of them are profusely illustrated. An exception, however, occurs in favour of Bentham's Bible, printed at Cambridge in 2 vols., folio, 1762, the whole of the edition, with the exception of about six copies, having been destroyed by fire. Collectors of New Testaments commence (when they can) with Tyndale's version of 1525, and seldom or never do more than look at any work bearing a later date than 1679.

It may, I think, be taken for granted that all Bibles and Testaments within the specified limits will certainly continue to increase in value. Many examples, however, which are offered for sale are either imperfect, or, what is worse, have been rebound and cut down in the process. These for the most part bear date between the years 1616-80, and sell for a few shillings each. The best book for collectors of old Bibles to study is published by Eyre and Spottiswoode at 10s. 6d. The author—Mr. J. R. Dore—is the first living expert on this difficult branch of bibliography, and has made it a life study.

9. Works on natural history are nearly all illustrated. In fact, the very nature of the subject imperatively demands that such should be the case. A botanical or ornithological work, for example, without illustrations, is of very little use from a practical point of view; and so well is the force of this recognised, that nearly all biological treatises are furnished with plates, which in many instances are found coloured. There seems to be little doubt that works on natural history, in order to hold their own in the market, *must* have the plates coloured. Those which are destitute of

plates, or have them uncoloured, have been decreasing in value for some time, and I do not see how they can recover their position. Works of the kind are, however, very rarely met with casually, and under any circumstances always command their value, which on the whole seems to be stationary. As one exception at least may always be confidently anticipated to every rule, it may noted that clean and good copies of Yarrell's be " British Birds " and " British Fishes," Bewick's " British Birds " and " Quadrupeds," particularly when the examples are on large paper, are increasing in value, even although none of the cuts are ever found coloured.

10. Works relating to antiquarian subjects are much in the same position, so far as regards their pecuniary value and the probability of their increasing in price. Books on armour, ancient dresses and costumes, sculpture, marbles, pottery, numismatology, stained glass, mosaics, cameos, tablets, vases, ancient monuments, brasses, heraldry, and similar subjects, are nearly always furnished with coloured illustrations. Where the contrary proves to be the case, the value may confidently be expected to decline. When, however, the plates are coloured, it should remain stationary for some time to come. The exceptions to this rule are few, and occur almost entirely in connection with very old works, which

are valued primarily as examples of early printing. These are, of course, very highly prized whatever the state of the woodcuts may be, or even if there are no illustrations at all. In heraldic books it is customary to announce the proper armorial colourings in the printed description of the quarterings, and works of this class are not often emblazoned. When they are, however, the value is correspondingly increased.

Works on archæology and general antiquities, referring chiefly to architectural remains, cathedral antiquities, monastic surveys, and the like, are sometimes illustrated and sometimes not. In either event the value appears to be stationary, and I do not think is at all likely to increase—at any rate for the present. Antiquarians of the peripatetic sort are a very limited class, and the literature they affect is seldom seen outside their own library walls, the London sale-rooms, or the shops of the larger booksellers.

11. Topographical works were at one time more valuable than they are now, but of late years the interest in them has somewhat revived. The larger and more expensive works—nearly all in folio—must, as a rule, be paid for; and it is safe to say that the person who does not know their worth has yet to be found. The truth is that the better class of topographical works carry with them their old reputation, and the

tendency, if anything, is to overvalue them. It is, however, quite usual to find octavo books offered for sale at a few pence, or perhaps shillings, each; and when I say that everyone of these is rising slowly, but none the less surely, in the market, the collector will perhaps see the advisability of accumulating as many as can be got at a reasonable price. Even if the full present value is paid, the investment should by no means be a bad one.

12. It has already been pointed out that classical works—by which I mean the productions of the Greek and Latin authors of antiquity—are just now at a discount. Not many years ago their value was five or six times as great as it is now. Indeed, so lightly are they esteemed, that numbers of them may be seen in the booksellers' shops awaiting a customer almost at any price. These remarks do not, however, apply to the *editiones principes*, or first editions, nearly all of which were printed during the latter quarter of the 15th or the first quarter of the 16th centuries, and are for the most part very valuable. Here again these early editions are valued for reasons other than the purity of their text. On the other hand, most of the productions of Aldus Manutius, of the Elzevirs, and nearly all the English-printed works of this class, more particularly the 18th

century editions, have fallen in value to an extent almost incredible, and that within the past ten or fifteen years. I cannot think, however, that the depression is likely to continue for long, and it might be worth the while of the reader to set about collecting works of this class. Only the other day I saw a copy of Combe's edition of Horace, in two vols., 4to, 1792, nicely bound in vellum, with gilt edges, awaiting a purchaser at 2s. How many days it had stood on the bookseller's shelf I know not: it is probably there yet; but this I do know, that thirty years ago the work would have been considered dirt cheap, not at 2s., but at £1 or more.

In the days of the great bibliographer the Rev. T. F. Dibdin, classical works were held to supply the appropriate literature for gentlemen of learning, and what Griswold calls "elegant leisure." Dibdin even wrote a book entitled "Introduction to the Greek and Latin Classics," and that such treatise should now be tolerably scarce, while many, or indeed most, of the numerous editions he so laboriously describes are just the reverse, is a curious satire on the times in which we live. Dibdin's book will be found indispensable to the classical collector— with this caution, that no reliance whatever can be placed on the author's estimate either of the scarcity or value of a single work he catalogues.

He teaches his readers, however, to discriminate between good and bad editions, for it goes without saying that there are a vast number of the latter in the market which never were of the slightest value and never will be.

The editions of the classics printed by Aldus Manutius at Venice are all of high quality, those of the Elzevirs at Leyden and Amsterdam, just the reverse. The former, himself a splendid classical scholar, criticised every word which issued from his press, and even kept a staff of experts to make assurance doubly sure; the Elzevirs blindly copied whatever came in their way, from Homer and Virgil downwards, and they seem to have not only copied mistakes, but to have made many original ones of their own. Nevertheless, the productions of the Elzevirs were always esteemed more highly by book-men than those of Aldus; for they excelled all other printers in the beauty of their type and the general get-up of the little volumes they turned out in such quantities. Many of these are to be seen on the book-stalls, but it is rare to find one that has not been cut down or otherwise maltreated   That the value of these works depends chiefly upon their measurement in millemètres, about 25½ of which go to the inch, is sufficient reason for avoiding mutilated specimens.

On the whole, I am of opinion that all classical works, but chiefly those from the presses of Aldus Manutius and the Elzevirs, as well as all the English-printed editions of the 18th century which possess a classical reputation, will shortly come into favour again. Should this surmise be warranted by the facts, there will be more money gained and lost over the works of the classical authors than over any other description of book whatsoever. Present prices are so low, future prices may again be so high, that the margin will be of the widest. Doubtless the persons to gain will be the dealers, for they are overstocked, and in all probability the quotations for works of this description will leap up at a bound, for they fell mysteriously in the same way.

13. If anyone were to search industriously for a bad investment, he could not possibly find a worse than theological and technical works afford. I do not mean to say that all books so classified are necessarily worthless; on the contrary, some few of them are both rare and valuable. Even a volume of sermons may be an object of intense interest to the book-hunter if the contents are in any way associated with a religious revolution in which the author was a prominent figure. Thus the works in the original of Luther, of any of the Marian martyrs, or of John Knox, would run a good chance of being snapped up

within a short time of being exposed for sale at a price less than they were worth.

The sermons of Manning and Newman always sell well, for obvious reasons ; but in hardly a single case out of many thousands are theological treatises of any kind worth much more than the paper on which they are printed.

Technical works are in the same position, unless perfectly new or very old, *i.e.*, of the 17th century at least. Nothing deteriorates in value so quickly as scientific treatises, and many of them are obsolete almost from the day of publication. This is the case with all cyclopædias, which, however good, begin to decrease in value immediately they are completed. In like manner a technical work on electricity, or ship-building, has a very short life. In time it may become too great a curiosity to be ignored, and so rank with the Marquess of Worcester's "A Century of the Names and Scantlings of such Inventions as I can Call to Mind," which was published so long ago as 1663, or the older book which Solomon de Caus published in 1615, under the title of *Les Raisons des Forces Mouvantes avec diverses Machines tant utiles que puissantes*, and which probably enlightened the Marquess of Worcester not a little, though the author was confined as a madman for writing it. In 200 years many things may happen, but not for us.

My advice to the reader is to avoid all books of this class, *i.e.*, theological and technical, unless they can be regarded as curiosities ; or, in the case of theological works, happen to be written by some notorious champion of his faith who lived, and perhaps died, for the principles he laid down.

14. In searching among large quantities of old books the reader may sometimes come across little pieces, frequently of doubtful merit, written by men who subsequently became famous. For instance, Charles Lamb once wrote a fairy tale, called "Prince Dorus ; or, Flattery Put Out of Countenance," which was published by Godwin in 1811. A copy of this little pamphlet—for it is nothing else—sold not long ago for £30. The same author, in conjunction with his sister, also wrote "Poetry for Children" in 1809, and "Mrs. Leicester's School" in the same year. A good copy of the former is worth £40 or thereabouts, and of the latter about £20. There is nothing in these productions which would commend either of them to a critic, but nevertheless they are very hard to procure. I once saw a fair copy of "Mrs. Leicester's School" in a second-hand furniture shop: the price was 4d., and I passed it by. Many years have elapsed since then, but I have never seen another, at any price.

In adjudicating on little pieces by famous

authors, the only plan is to consider the subsequent reputation of the writer, and to judge
the value of the work from that standpoint. This
is more often than not a very difficult matter,
for it is seldom that any author's name is mentioned on the title-pages of the crude and
ill-digested works submitted to the public in
youthful days. I know of no other plan, however;
and if knowledge is wanting there is no way
of acquiring it but by reading, and experiencing
an occasional disappointment similar to the one
related in connection with "Mrs. Leicester's
School."

15. Accidental books are those which are
brought into prominence for the time being by
reason of public attention being specially drawn
to the subject to which they relate. It would
be difficult to find a more apt or appropriate
illustration of what is meant than that afforded
by the well-known Bradshaw's Railway Guide,
which some few years ago was not looked upon
as being worth the notice of the collector. When,
however, the fiftieth year of publication came
round, and attention was drawn to the fact in
the press, the earlier issues immediately began
to be sought after. In June last year a copy of
the first edition of Bradshaw's Time Tables, dated
" 10th mo., 19th, 1839," sold for no less than £11.

Again, during the Jubilee year much interest ·

was manifested in the Coronation number of the *Sun*, which was printed in gilt letters in 1838. Two or three shillings would have purchased a copy of this five years ago, but directly the Jubilee celebrations were announced the price rose to 10s. or 12s. At the present time it stands at about 5s., but when another coronation takes place it will probably reach £1, or near it.

These two examples afford cogent evidence of the liability of the public to be swayed even in their choice of books by the events of the day. So sure as a subject, no matter what, takes a firm hold of the popular mind, so certainly will books which treat of it rise both in importance and value. It is obvious that great results may be achieved by looking ahead, and so ascertaining what event is likely to become prominent in the near future.

16. Works on ancient and modern philosophy, jurisprudence and medicine, philology and criticism, parliamentary procedure and practice, including reports of debates and journals of both houses, may be classed under one heading. They are works which do not often change hands, and vary but little in price. Books of this class to be of value must be the best of their kind. Old law and medical works are, as a rule, worse than useless; they are misleading, and the pecuniary value attaching to them is consequently trivial

in the extreme. Reports of proceedings in the courts, statutes, medical treatises tinged with astrology, and old surgical works written by practitioners who effected a radical change in professional opinion are, however, exceptions. These, as a rule, sell well, and are likely to maintain their value in the future.

17. Geographical works, strictly so called, are worthless unless quite new or exceedingly old. In the former case they are useful; in the latter they take a high position as curiosities, in which event they are, and have been for some time, rising in value. We must remember that old books of voyages and travels are distinctly geographical in their nature, and many of these are excessively rare and valuable. Books relating to the American Continent have already been referred to as being well-nigh impossible to obtain, and it may be taken as an axiom that any book of travels, dated during the 17th century or at any time previous, are certain to be worth far more in the near future than they are now. Thus, the voyages of Sir Francis Drake, Esquemeling's "Bucaniers of America," and all Eden's and Hakluyt's works are becoming scarcer every day. Good copies of Cook's voyages— an 18th century book of course — are in the same position. Nearly all these old books of discovery have, however, been reprinted or pub-

lished in an abridged or "improved" form, and
of these later editions the reader must beware.
They are mostly found in small octavo and
dated between 1750 and 1820, and illustrated
with old and worn-out plates. Their value, from
any point of view, is simply *nil*. Atlases, if old
(dated say before 1700), are rising in value; all
others are distinctly deteriorating. On the whole,
the only kind of geographical works worth collecting for future purposes are 15th, 16th, and
17th century voyages, travels, and maps.

18. Historical and biographical works are somewhat in the same position as geographical treatises.
They must be quite new or else very old, and
they must also be of the best quality. Hundreds
and thousands of trivial books of this class litter
the stalls, and are to be bought for a few pence
each. They consist for the most part of inferior
editions of the works of famous authors, bad
translations, or abridgments got up for sale at
a cheap rate. These worthless books are mostly
dated during the 18th century, though some
were published at the beginning of this. Historical and biographical works do not afford
much scope for the collector, though some, such
as the old chronicles, are valuable, and may
reasonably be expected to become more so in
course of time.

19. Of recent years great curiosity has been

evinced by almost every class of society in books on astrology, geomancy, white or black magic, witchcraft, mesmerism, and other occult or mystical sciences. By far the greater number are in Latin, but in whatever language they may be, there can be no doubt of their great importance. It is said that large quantities are collected for export to America, where the value is, if anything, greater than it is here. Whatever the facts in this respect, it seems to be beyond question that the past five years has witnessed a rapid rise in works of this class. Even the new books continually being published by one or two firms who have made this particular branch of literature a speciality, sell rapidly and well. In my opinion, all works of this class, old or new, will continue to rise in the market, and at present offer one of the best investments it is possible for the collector to secure.

CHAPTER V.

UNCONSIDERED TRIFLES.

THE greatest of Shakespearian scholars, the late Mr. Halliwell-Phillipps, narrates that when he first began hunting for old books at the various stalls, black-letter volumes were as plentiful as blackberries. These for the most part he found in very unlikely places—often indeed among masses of rubbish exposed for sale in boxes outside the booksellers' windows. About the year 1840, he began to turn his attention to the more special work of collecting Shakespeare quartos, and steadily accumulated a considerable number, which included no less than three examples of the very rare "Romeo and Juliet" of 1609. In fact, more early quarto Shakespeares were at one time or another in that gentleman's possession than are ever likely to fall to the lot of a single individual again, while his collection of black-letter tracts, many of the highest degree of rarity, was extraordinarily large and important. All these books, so dear to the heart of the modern collector, Mr. Halliwell-Phillipps, had picked up here and there for trifling sums. When we, perchance fired by the recital of his successes, seek to follow his example, little but disappointment rewards our exertions. Sometimes a rare volume is met with, generally when least expected; but more often than not a protracted search round and about the book-stalls reveals nothing—absolutely nothing—worth carrying away. There are ready reckoners, volumes of sermons and exhortations in plenty, a spelling-book or two, and a varied assortment of school-books, multitudes of pamphlets on subjects of limited interest, and bad and imperfect editions of standard works without end. Among all this chaff a single ear of wheat is sometimes discovered, and that is all there is to remind us of the days when the threshing-floor was piled high with golden grain.

As matters stand, it is perfectly obvious that the book-hunter must make up his mind to almost ignore the fashion as it exists to-day, and to peer into the future, to collect for the future, to talk chiefly of the future. This is no new thing for Mr. Halliwell-Phillipps, and many others possessed of tastes like his did the same.

Quite likely enough, people will some day sigh for the time when Sir Walter Scott's originals could be bought for half-a-crown each, and may call these the halcyon days of book-collecting. If so, they will think no more highly of our discretion than we do of that of the Manchester bookseller, who, thirty years ago or so, sold a second folio to Mr. James Crossley for a shilling.

The fact is that no days are golden until they are beyond recall, and in our journeyings to and fro we must not now expect to discover vast treasures at the price of an old song, like the first perfect Aldine Virgil which the Duke of Hamilton and Mr. Beckford pursued fruitlessly all their lives. None of the old collectors did that habitually, they bought *what no one else would buy at the time*, and when their forecast of the future state of the market turned out to be correct, and their purchases began to be envied, they posed as famous book-hunters. We must do the same, even though nothing but time can justify our choice. We, or at any rate most of us, cannot afford to give £300, or even half that number of shillings, for some fashionable tract, and it is folly to go specially in search of what we know can only be discovered very occasionally.

The longer the subject of book-collecting is considered, the plainer it will appear that we have little to hope from following the fashion, unless, indeed, money is of no account. Not that we should close our eyes to what is going on around us. On the contrary, quickness of perception, and an aptitude for taking any opportunity which Providence may see fit to throw in our way, is part of the book-hunter's training, and he would be a sorry hunter indeed without these essentials to success. Accept any rarity which presents itself, but do not search specially for it ; leave the popular taste of the hour to be gratified by the exertions of others, and do not contribute to what is at its best an expensive luxury. This advice points away from the beaten track in the direction of new paths, some of which, if well chosen, may eventually become thoroughfares.

Although books which are excessively rare and valuable may be out of the reach of most people, there are doubtless hundreds and thousands of desirable works awaiting purchasers at this moment in the City of London alone. Some, as the reader will have gathered, are of no particular value to-day, though they may be eagerly sought after a year or two hence. Others are even now worth more than the price put upon them, and will speedily be bought up. A third class consists of books which in themselves are nearly or perhaps absolutely worthless, but are yet of great importance by reason of special circumstances which surround them.

Some few months ago a well-known collector of old Bibles came across a fragment of

Coverdale's version of the Bible in 16mo. ($3\frac{7}{8}$in. by $2\frac{5}{8}$ in.), hitherto entirely unknown. The discovery constituted one of the most interesting events which had occurred for a long time in the bibliographical world, and was made quite accidentally. The fragment in question consisted of thirty-two pages, containing a portion of the Book of Proverbs (from chapter xii. to chapter xv.), and had been used to pack or line the covers of a 4to copy of " An Abstract of the Penal Statutes, Collected by Fardinando Palton, of Lincolnes Inne, Gentleman," printed by Christopher Barker early in the reign of Elizabeth. Of course until this comparatively worthless book was stripped of its covers the fragment would be entirely hidden from the public gaze, and so it had come to pass that for two or three hundred years generation after generation of book-hunters had passed the law book by, or perhaps retained it for a brief space on their shelves, without a thought.

Not so long ago, I bought for a few pence a battered old volume, printed at Lyons in 1546. It was nothing but an exposition of the Roman Law of Contracts by Andreas Alciatus, of Milan, and from a pecuniary point of view of no importance. What struck me was the quaint vellum binding, and the strange appearance of the " bands"; those pieces of leather, cardboard, or other suitable substance glued to the back of a book previous to covering. In this instance the bands proved to consist of strips of parchment, part of an old illuminated manuscript, which had thus been sacrificed in days when manuscripts were more common, and of less importance than printed books.

Incredible damage seems to have been done in old times by ignorant or careless binders, who frequently packed or bound their books with anything that came first to hand. Hence some of these fragments, as in the case of Coverdale's Bible above mentioned, turn out to be of exceptional interest, and sometimes of very great importance in the literary world, and care should consequently be taken to thoroughly search every old book which for any reason may be supposed to be padded or made up of fragments in the binding.

The presence of an autograph in any part of an old or indeed modern work will also sometimes invest it with a degree of importance it could never have acquired under other circumstances. Many signatures are difficult to read, and so are frequently passed by persons who might be expected to know better; some, on the other hand, though clear enough, are scribbled not on the title page, which may perhaps be considered the most suitable place, but in out of the way portions of the volume, and so escape notice altogether. At one time I found an inscription and autograph of Ben Jonson on a blank leaf of a mutilated copy of Florus, at another I bought for a shilling an old book of Statutes with the signature of Bradshaw the Regicide written clearly enough on the title.

Such instances are by no means rare, though, as a matter of fact, the signatures of Ben Jonson and Bradshaw are not often met with. When, however, we consider that a book may pass through a hundred hands during the course of its existence, and that some famous men have had large libraries and were remarkably fond of writing their names in, or perhaps even of annotating their books, it is obvious that there must be a large number which are distinctly worth searching for.

Hence it follows that the experienced book-hunter has acquired the habit of opening every book he sees ; he does so somewhat abstractedly in many cases, but the early training which prompts the act is apparent in every gesture.

Some of the books which have belonged to famous men are curious as well as important, but most, unless authenticated with a signature, can never hope to be identified. Charles Lamb, for example, was a voracious reader, and handled his books without the slightest regard to their preservation. Writing to Coleridge, he says, "A book reads the better which is our own and has been so long known to us that we know the topography of its blots and dog's-ears, and can trace the dirt in it to having read it at tea with buttered muffins, or over a pipe, which I think is the maximum." Personally, I should think that the climax of untidiness which Lamb thus modestly charges to his account is about the minimum of what he was capable, for I once had one of his books, which was a sight to behold. Dog's-ears and blots and "dirt" of every description defaced its pages, and whole lines of text had been scored out, sometimes in ink, at others in pencil. In an ordinary case, of course, the book would not have been improved, but the peculiar circumstances invested it with an interest and importance it would be hard to exaggerate.

Montaigne, it appears, was in the habit of writing a sort of criticism on the merits of every book he read; this he wrote in the book itself. Voltaire did the same, and in his case it made no difference whether the volume belonged to himself or anyone else. Young, the poet, dog-eared every leaf on which appeared any passage which struck his fancy, and his library was choked with half-closed books. John Selden, the antiquary, used his spectacles as book-markers, and these were found by dozens after his death.

Wordsworth was as bad as Lamb in his treatment of books—perhaps worse; for Coleridge, who ought to know, expressed the opinion that "You might just as well turn a bear into a tulip garden as let Wordsworth loose in your library."

"There are men whose handling of your books makes you tremble. It is told even of the great Professor Wilson that he would stalk into Blackwood's shop and, disdainful of implements, would rip open the leaves of uncut books with his great fingers."

A book-collector of the graver sort—that is to say one who knows more than the mere outsides of the volumes which line his walls—has need of all the knowledge he can acquire, for many books which look so uninviting may nevertheless be invested with a halo of romance. To many persons they will seem worthless, but this is far from being the case if only the link of identity can be forged to the personality of some famous owner of a bygone day. As a rule only an autograph can accomplish this satisfactorily. There is here a field of enterprise in which not a few collectors of the present day have been extraordinarily successful.

Volumes of tracts which, in the vast majority of cases, are found to consist of sermons or theological pamphlets, sometimes contain other pieces of a more valuable description, which, on being detached from the body of the work and cleaned and rebound, may fairly be said to have been rescued from oblivion.

An experienced book-hunter never permits a volume of tracts to pass through his hands without examination. In most cases it will be found that some attempt has been made at classification, but this is not always the case. Occasionally an unimportant sermon will be found bound up with other pieces of quite a different description. In this way many rare tracts have been discovered, some of them even unique, while of others only a few copies have been known to be in existence. At one time it was the usual practice to bind up a sufficient number of pamphlets to make the volume even in bulk with others which already stood upon the shelf. Those which were not then of importance were gathered up and bound together, and perhaps for many years might be regarded merely as useful for filling up spaces which would otherwise be left vacant.

Time works wonders in the book-world as elsewhere, and so it occasionally happens that the despised volume of two hundred years ago may be found to be now worth more than its weight in gold.

The subject of mutilated and imperfect books has already been referred to, though very incidentally. Some collectors like to buy their books by instalments, so to speak, and find more genuine pleasure in "making up" an edition than in buying one entire. Let us assume for a moment that a set of Pope's works, 1754 or 1757, in ten volumes, can be bought second-hand for as many shillings. It does not follow from this that two or three volumes out of the set would be worth a proportionate sum, viz., 2s. or 3s. On the contrary, the value would be much less. Again, a volume which is deficient either as regards its leaves or its plates is not worth anything like what it would have been if complete. The law of proportion does not hold good in these instances, because the trouble which would be involved in completing the imperfect set or book, as the case may be, would be out of all proportion to the advantage to be ultimately gained. Nevertheless, many collectors think that in their case the contrary rule prevails, and are prepared to buy any incomplete set or book at a small price, on the chance of being able sooner or later to add the remaining volumes, or the missing leaves or plates. So far as I can see, the only advantage to be gained by following this system is that the cost is very materially reduced.

If time were of no object, and room could be found for the very extensive collection which would have to be made as a ground work for future operations, then the plan would be advantageous rather than otherwise; but when we consider that a missing volume may not be found for years, and a missing plate, which must necessarily be procured from some other work, itself imperfect in other respects, perhaps not at all, it is difficult to see in what the advantage really and in the long run consists. I have known several book-hunters who adopted this plan for a time, but one only who persistently followed it through a long life. When his books came to be sold, it was found that time had curbed his hand, and had been much too short to enable him to complete even a section of his library, truly described by a hunter after unconsidered trifles as a thing of shreds and patches.

In some cases, and particularly when operations are conducted on a limited scale, it may be advantageous, or even desirable to "make up" a book, rather than to spend a large sum of money on the purchase of an entire copy. This is a question of individual taste, of time, and of depth of purse, which each can answer for himself. Under all circumstances and in every instance, however, it is better to have an imperfect book than one which has been cut down by the binder. The former *may* be completed, the latter can never be anything better than it is—an object incapable of reparation from the very nature of the case, and altogether discredited.

CHAPTER VI.

ROUGH DIAMONDS.

SO close and searching is the hunt for old books of a certain kind, that every out-of-the-way stall and shop in the metropolis is regularly and systematically visited by the dealers or their agents.

Mr. G. A. Sala states that most of his interesting, curious, or valuable books have been picked up from the costermongers' barrows which line the New Cut on a Sunday morning; and certainly the presence of the crowd which perambulates that and other thoroughfares of the metropolis where the peripatetic dealers are in the habit of congregating, would seem to argue that not only must there must be something of interest to detain them, but also that the chance of acquiring a bargain must be remote in the extreme after a certain hour of the day.

The first hypothesis is more or less justified,

the second only partially so, for the majority
of those who are found turning over books on
the stalls are either actuated by idle curiosity
or in search of some work, generally of an
educational kind, which they may happen to
want at the time. From such bookworms as
these there is little to fear, for in all probability they would not be able to identify an
uncommon work, even though they should take
it up and examine its pages from cover to
cover. They would see nothing of importance,
for example, in the "Scholemaster" of Roger
Ascham, the tutor of Queen Elizabeth, valuable
not so much from the nature of its contents—
which, as a matter of fact, are now but seldom
read—as on account of its being the first important work on education in the English
language.

So far as regards the "jackals," however,
the case is different. The men indicated by this
predatory title make a business of thoroughly
searching all the stalls, either on their own
account or as agents for the booksellers, with
whom they are occasionally connected. They
are, as a rule, good judges not only of old
books, but of china, prints, and all articles which
may conveniently be classed under the head of
bric-à-brac ; and everything of this nature which
comes within their ken is carefully scrutinised

and bought up, should it disclose the slightest margin of profit.

I once knew a "jackal" who kept an old curiosity shop in one of the slums off Drury Lane. He was ill-conditioned, dirty, and, as a rule, taciturn and surly, but withal one of the best judges of antiquities, including old books, if they can be so classed, in all London. His shop was a mere storehouse for the numerous articles he picked up during the rounds which occupied half his time, the other half being spent in reporting his purchases to likely customers, whom he called on personally with a list of his gleanings. At his death his shop was found to be stocked with the accumulations of years—a miscellaneous assortment of the most curious and out-of-the-way articles, procured for the most part from street stalls and the shops of the marine store dealers.

Into the nets of such men as these is swept nearly every unconsidered trifle which awaits a purchaser, and the amateur requires all his wits and needs to be up very early in the morning, and that in its two-fold sense, if he would hold even a semblance of his own against such professional competition.

It has already been pointed out that a large proportion of the books which may be styled "valuable"—that is to say of some value beyond a nominal sum—are easily judged from their appearance; but there are many which, although they look mean and worthless, are, nevertheless, of the greatest possible interest to the collector, being scarce, and, for various reasons, the majority of which it would perhaps be impossible to analyse, of considerable importance from a pecuniary point of view.

I am not aware that a list of what may be called "rough diamonds" has as yet been compiled, nor could even a tolerably complete one be attempted within the compass of a small book. The advantage of some such list would, however, be exceedingly great to the collector, for he would then be able to draw his own conclusions with regard to other works of a similar description. Books which are old, perhaps battered, but yet complete, and frequently "uncut," mean in appearance, and seemingly worthless, are just the kind that are likely to be met with for a small sum. Inferior-looking themselves, they are often found in inferior localities—in dirty shops among masses of rags and bones, scrap iron, and other abominations. The reader will not find them in the main thoroughfares, except at a price.

It is no use haunting the shops of the recognised dealers, after the manner of the American gentleman, who, not so long ago, "rushed," as he graphically described it, out of Holywell Street into the Strand with a book for which he had just paid double its value, under the erroneous impression that he had at last acquired a genuine bargain. Not that rare books are unknown in such localities, or that dealers are infallible— far from it; but as a rule they know their business, and very rarely allow anything of value to slip through their fingers. An ignorant or careless apprentice may certainly fill the four-penny box with the first lot of books that comes to hand, the proprietor may be ill and unable to attend to his business himself—he may even make a gross mistake. The amateur's chances are, however, in exact proportion to the infrequence of such occurrences, and are the result of the purest accident. Money is picked up in the road sometimes, but always when unsought for; so it is with valuable books in the shop of a dealer of repute.

The rough diamonds which it is even yet worth while to search for cannot very well be referred to separately, for their number is far too great for detailed notice in any book but one specially devoted to cataloguing them. Nor indeed would that be the proper way of imparting the required information, for the best catalogue could not be otherwise than deficient, while its enormous bulk would render it unwieldly, and in the last degree difficult of access. The only satisfactory method of distinguishing one book from another, and judging at a glance, of its value and importance, is to assign it to some particular class.

A bookseller who seems to fix the value of a work so easily may never have seen it before, or even heard of it, but he knows by intuition whether it is likely to be scarce, and consequently worth buying. The mental process which leads up to the opinion he forms is based on a system of classification which becomes more and more complicated as his experience matures.

So must it be with the judgment of the amateur, and the best way of exercising it is to take a good bookseller's catalogue and go through each item, carefully noting the prices affixed, and endeavouring to assign a reason for their being high or the reverse. It will be found that nothing is valued at random, and that the books are not tumbled together without any attempt at arrangement, as so many persons seem to suppose.

The following classification covers nearly the whole ground the amateur will have to tread in his search for books which have little to indicate their value, so far as appearance is concerned. They are for the most part scarce, though not hopelessly so, in fact they are just the kind likely to reward a patient search.

Any old books of facetiæ of the 17th or early part of the 18th centuries—such, for example, as the "Wit Interpreter," 1671; "Witt's Recreations Augmented with Ingenious Conceits," 1667; "The Wit's Academy," 1704; "Joe Miller's Jests, or The Wit's Vade Mecum," 1738, or the second edition of 1739, "Polly Peachum's Jests," 1728; or any old works recounting the adventures and sayings of Till Owleglasse, Will Summers, Archie Armstrong, and other famous jesters.

Any volumes of poetry of the 17th century, no matter what the edition may be, or of the 18th or 19th centuries if first or sometimes early editions. Attention should be directed not so much to the quality of the text as to the reputation acquired by the author; and as that is high or low, so as a rule will be the value of the early editions of his works. Sometimes, as already explained, an author's name is so famous that it will carry value to several editions beyond the first, though this is not often the case.

In this catagory are the first edition of Burns' works, Kilmarnock, 1786, and the first Edinburgh and London editions of 1787; the poems of Byron and Scott (though these sell for small

sums at present, even by the booksellers);
the poems of Ada Isaacs Menken, entitled
"Infelicia," 1868; first or even early editions of
any living poets of the first rank, such as
Tennyson, Swinburne, Arnold, Lewis or William
Morris, and George Meredith; or of modern
poets, such as Browning, Tom Moore, Tom Hood,
Wordsworth, or Longfellow. All verse printed
during the 17th century is valuable, and to this
rule there are but few exceptions. Modern
poetry by unknown authors is valueless, and not
worth collecting on the chance of its becoming
popular, even though written by a vain-glorious
poet like the one who boasted that his works would
be read when Dryden and Pope were forgotten :
"But not till then," added his candid friend.
All modern reprints should be avoided, unless
published by one of the learned societies, such
as the Roxburghe Club and a few others, or at
the private presses of Strawberry Hill, Middle
Hill, Darlington, or Lee Priory.

Any book of the 16th century, printed in any
part of Great Britain, no matter who by or on
what subject. This is in accordance with a rule
which never fails when rambling round and about
the book-stalls, where the prices may be expected

to be low.   Scotch-printed books of this era
are very rare, though by no means hopelessly
so.   Any works relating to the American continent and printed in any language during the
16th and 17th centuries are of the highest degree
of importance.

Any old plays of the 17th century, nearly all
of which are in small quarto, or any works whatever of that era which contain a woodcut in
any part of them.   Any original editions of the
Elizabethan dramatists, whether they consist of
stage plays or not, are always worth collecting.
The works of Shirley, Dekker, Ford, Massinger,
Greene, Beaumont and Fletcher, and many other
writers of this age, are of considerable importance.
Another book of this era, though of an entirely
different nature, is Burton's "Anatomy of
Melancholy," which supplied Milton with the
material for two of his finest poems and innumerable authors of lesser note with most of their
learning.   Inseparably associated with this work
is Timothy Bright's "A Treatise of Melancholy,"
1586, rendered doubly important, inasmuch as
the author was a noted man in his day, being
the inventor of the modern system of shorthand.

Any tracts or pamphlets relating to theological controversy, provided they are dated at any time during the 16th century and by such well-known characters as Gardiner, Bishop of Winchester, Latimer, any of the Marian Martyrs, Bullinger, Martin Luther, or John Knox. It will be remembered that volumes of sermons, which litter the bookstalls in such vast quantities, are never of any value, unless they can be brought within the rule and so ascribed to some great religious reformer. All theological books are practically governed by the same rule, viz., in estimating the value of works of this class look first to the man who wrote them, and afterwards at the book itself. No matter how learned the latter may be, it will have no value if the author is unknown.

Any old books on angling, and most modern ones too for the matter of that. The great prize here is the first edition, or failing that, one of the earlier editions of Walton's "Angler," first published in 1653, and of whose author Byron wrote :

> Angling, too, that solitary vice,
> Whatever Isaac Walton sings and says,
> The quaint, old, cruel coxcomb in his gullet
> Should have a hook, and a small trout to pull it.

Just now great interest is manifested in all works of a sporting nature, and no little book or pamphlet should be allowed to pass which relates to angling, archery, cock-fighting, bear- or bull-baiting, badger-drawing, boxing, hawking, or hunting. Most of these are perhaps somewhat pretentious in appearance, and consequently seldom to be met with casually; others, how-ever, are just the reverse.

Greek and Latin classics, though at a very low ebb just at present, may confidently be expected to improve. Should they do so, the rise will be rapid. Only the best editions can safely be speculated in; the rest are mere rubbish which can never be of any greater value than they are now. School-books should be avoided, as they are of no pecuniary value. To this rule there are but few exceptions which cannot be brought within the provisions of the following paragraph. The most noticeable of them consists of very old books like the early editions of "Cocker's Arithmetic," most of which are extraordinarily rare.

Any children's books of the earlier part of the century, particularly those published by M. J.

Godwin "at the Juvenile Library, No. 41,
Skinner Street," about the year 1810. Many of
these little books were written by Charles
Lamb and his sister, and these are now very
rare and valuable. Such are "Poetry for
Children," 1809, worth £30 or £40; "Mrs.
Leicester's School, 1809," worth £20 or £25,
and "Prince Dorus," 1811, of at least an equal
value. All children's books of about these dates
are rare, especially when in good condition, as
vast quantities must have been dog-eared and
thumbed, or perhaps torn to pieces by their
juvenile owners.

Any theatrical publications of the earlier
portion of the present century, such as "Actors
by Daylight; or, Pencillings in the Pit," 1838;
"Actors by Gaslight," 1838; "The Call Boy,"
1838; "The Critic, a Journal of Theatricals,"
&c., 1843-44. Any of the numerous pamphlets
relating to Miss Farren, afterwards Countess of
Derby, Madame Vestris, Bickerstaff, David
Garrick, and other famous actors, particularly if
scandalous or libellous, like the "Secret Memoirs
of Harriott Pumpkin (Harriet Mellon), from her
Infancy to her Seduction of, and subsequent
Marriage with, a Banker," &c., 1825, 8vo, a book

which was rigidly suppressed on its appearance, and is now worth some £8 or £10.

Original editions of famous novels of a bygone day, such as any of those by Samuel Richardson, or more particularly the better-known works of De Foe, Smollett, and Fielding, and in a minor degree those of Mrs. Radcliffe, Maturin, and "Monk" Lewis. Books in this class are not numerous, but they must be good uncut copies to realise their full value or to excite any amount of competition. Most of the copies offered for sale have, unfortunately, been rebound and cut down in the process.

Any works which treat of astrology, magic, witchcraft, mysticism or religious fanaticism, no matter in what language or when dated. Many, or more correctly most, of the older works on these subjects are in Latin, and not a few in 8vo or small 4to, like the Malleus Malificarum of Sprenger and Institor; the works of Agrippa; Artemidorus, who wrote of dreams and their interpretation; Artephius the alchemist; Behmen the mystic; Gadbury and Lilly the astrologers;

Grillandus, who classed heretics and sorcerers together and gave a damning history of both in the year 1536; some of the editions of the blasphemous Black Grimoire, which renders murder necessary to the performance of its rites, and of the " De Prestigiis Dæmonum " of Wierus the physician, who, together with Reginald Scot, braved the wrath of King James, though at a safe distance. All these, and many other books of the same kind, are occasionally met with in their battered sheepskin bindings, and all, without exception, are worthy of the earnest attention of the collector.

Such are some of the works which may occasionally be met with by those who are sufficiently persevering to search for them.

CHAPTER VII.

RULES TO FOLLOW.

VERY few of the books offered for sale, unless it be in the better-class shops, are in all respects perfect. Very often a plate will be missing, and the deficiency is perhaps not detected until the work comes to be compared with another copy known to be in the condition in which it left the publisher's hands. The want of a frontispiece, or even a title-page, is also a very usual blemish, for a number of people, at whose head was a certain depredating bookseller named John Bagford, used at one time to collect these, to the detriment of every volume they came across. Bagford's collection of title-pages, now in the British Museum, fills a large number of folios, constituting a monument to misguided energy which it would perhaps be impossible to match elsewhere. Another defect, and the commonest of all, must be placed to the debit of a long generation of ignorant or careless binders, who were accustomed to shave the edges of every book entrusted to them for re-binding. Any book thus treated falls in value on the instant, and the extent of the depreciation will depend upon the quantum of injury inflicted upon it. Occasionally we find that the binder's shears have cropped the very headlines, at other times the damage is not so great.

Some books are so excessively rare that copies are eagerly competed for regardless of the fact that they are badly "cropped," but such instances as these are the exceptions which prove the first of the rules it is necessary to learn, viz., that it is better on the whole to purchase an imperfect book than one which has been cut down by the binder. The reason of this is obvious. A missing plate, frontispiece, title-page, or leaf may be replaced, and often at a small cost, from another book, itself perhaps imperfect in other respects; but no power on earth can add a single millimètre to the edge of a sheet of paper which has been cut.

Of course, when books are offered for sale at a very low price, defects, whether of mutilation or imperfection, cannot be complained of, but when anything like the full value is asked, the greatest care should be exercised in order to see that no imperfections exist. In the vast majority of cases it is better to reject an imperfect book altogether than to take it at a slight reduction. As to a cropped work, it is well to remember that the normal value will have fallen from 15 per cent. to 75 per cent., or perhaps more, according to the extent of the injury.

Where compelled to guess at an edition or value, it must be remembered that where a work is reprinted away from its country of origin, it is seldom of importance. In cases where this rule does not hold good, it will generally be found that any value the work may have depends for its existence on the illustrations; or in very rare instances, on the excellent quality or rarity of the printing; or in rarer cases still, on the extraordinary reputation of the author, which carries its impress with it even abroad. A copy of any of Byron's works, for example, to be of value, must have been printed in England. No Scotch or Irish edition can be of any importance for itself alone. Also, French books reprinted in England, or *vice versâ*, can hardly be of any value; and the principle extends to every kind of book which, in common parlance, is a stranger to the country in which it sees the light. Some of the classical authors have been translated in this country, as Dryden translated Virgil, and Chapman, Homer; but in these cases the importance of the translation, combined with the fact that there were no original editions of the authors in question except in manuscript, is instrumental in creating an interest of a dual nature, one part of which centres in the classic, the other in the translation. In other words, the books must be regarded as entirely distinct, and each judged on its merits.

A third rule, and one which can be traced to a very recent origin, though the grounds upon which it is based, are perhaps not quite so apparent as they might be, has reference to the binding up of parts. It is well known that many of the works of Dickens, Thackeray, Lever, and other modern novelists, were originally issued in parts, and the rule in these cases is that to bind is to spoil. The parts should be preserved in a drop-case, and intact as they were issued; for if bound up, the value will fall considerably. As an instance, perhaps no better example could be given than Dickins's "Pickwick Papers," first published, it will be remembered, in 1837. A good set of the original parts cannot be got, even by auction, for much less than £9 or £10; whereas a bound uncut copy must be a very good one indeed to realise half the smaller sum. At the Mackenzie Sale held in March, 1889, a bound copy of the Pickwick Papers sold for no less than £22. The circumstances were highly exceptional, and yet must be present to a greater or less extent in every case where it is desired that nothing shall be lost by the act of binding. The book contained the two Buss plates, with the original wrappers and all the advertisements, specimens, &c., bound up separately in morocco extra by Rivière, one of the best binders of the age, and was, of course, absolutely uncut. In this, as in every other case, the binder's shears would have reduced the value to almost nothing.

As a corollary to this rule, the question of rebinding under any circumstances is one that frequently assumes considerable prominence. There is no doubt that it is advisable to retain the original covers as long as they will hold together; but if the work is of any value and *must* be rebound, only the best workmen should be employed for the purpose. This, though expensive, is essential. If expense is an object, it will be better to have the binding repaired, which in the vast majority of cases can easily be done.

In judging the value of any book, remember that intrinsic quality is the real basis of value, and that a bad or unknown author cannot have produced other than an unimportant book. The author may be known *quâ* author, or in any other capacity, just as the Earl of Rochester, whose poems in the original are so scarce and valuable, was known as an historical personage and an intimate friend of King Charles II.

We may be quite sure that modern collectors do not choose their books but upon some well-known and authoritative system of selection; and therefore, in judging of the importance of any book, it is necessary to ask in the first place, Who was the author? This may require extensive know ledge to answer, or it may not; but it must be replied to satisfactorily, notwithstanding.

Next comes the question, Is the edition a good one? Is it contemporary with the author, or, better still in most cases, original? Is it a mere translation of some foreign work, and, if so, who translated it? To what class does it belong, and is that class of importance? These and other necessary questions have already been enlarged on, and must be answered in every case where it is not known as a fact whether any particular book is of importance or not.

The contents of every bookstall of the common order will be found to consist chiefly of technical works, such as scientific books, educational works, and the like. The rule here is that none of these are of any value unless quite new (which is seldom, if ever, the case) or very old. In the former instance they may be worth half of the published price for purposes of reference; in the latter they may be very valuable as curiosities.

Thus " The Art of Cookery made Plain and Easy," 1747, folio, is valuable, for it is the first edition of Mrs. Glasse's well-known work, and as such, a curiosity. In like manner any of the earlier editions of Cocker's " Arithmetic," or the Marquess of Worcester's " A Century of the Names and Scantlings of such Inventions as I can Call to Mind," 1663, 8vo, are also curiosities, and consequently of value. In all these cases the author must be known, and this, of course, brings his book into prominence—a reversal possibly in many cases of the process by which he acquired his reputation, though the result, so far as we are concerned, is the same.

Another rule to be observed is that where a work consists of more than one volume, any one or more volumes out of the complete set is or are not of the same value *pro ratâ*. Thus we know that Grote's " History of Greece," 1884, is complete in twelve volumes, and worth, when well bound, £2 to £3 by auction, or, roughly speaking, about 5s. per volume. Six volumes out of the set would not, however, be worth 30s., nor three volumes, 15s.; for the trouble of collecting those which are missing would militate against the value very considerably. For this reason some collectors delight, as already explained, in " making up " their sets. They rank the trouble as a pleasure and an occupation of time which would otherwise hang heavily on their hands. From this point of view the practice may be justified, though the result is hardly ever satisfactory.

A collection of anything, no matter what, is rendered of greater relative importance, and consequently of greater value, as it approaches completion. This rule is well known and often followed by book-collectors, who not infrequently turn their attention to the accumulation of works by a certain author, or of a certain class, thus stamping the collection as a whole with an importance which perhaps cannot be claimed for the majority of the books which compose it. The late Mr. James Crossley, President of the Cheetham Society, though an enthusiastic all-round buyer, got together during the course of his long life a fine assortment of the works of De Foe. These were worth far more in the mass than if the value of each book had been taken singly and added up to form the total. In collecting the " De Imitatione Christi " of Thomas à Kempis, Edmund Waterton had, up to the time of his death, succeeded in bringing together between 1100 and 1200 different editions in various languages, and for some years before his death he had been engaged on a history of the book.

From this point of view a collection of the most worthless books may become an object of interest, assuming only that it approaches completion. In this, however, as in every other case, it will be found that there will be some editions which will baffle for a time the most active search, and it is these which impress a value on the whole.

The final rule to which it will be necessary to call attention is of great importance, as affording a reason of the prevailing mania for collecting first editions of popular authors. All conditions being equal, a first edition is always of more value than the ones which follow, because in the vast majority of cases it has been revised by the author. So says the collector; and as he is master of the situation—the "verie two eyes," so to speak, of the whole system which regulates the traffic in books—his word is law and must be obeyed. On this rule depends the whole future of the book market, so far as original editions are concerned, and on this will depend the future reputation of many a work now hardly noticed at all. The original editions of Sir Walter Scott's poems and novels have already been instanced, and when the collector is true to the reason which at present he only partially obeys, these and many other works which are at present tossed lightly aside will assume the position to which they are justly entitled. A reason once demonstrated must form part and for ever remain of the spirit of truth.

CHAPTER VIII.

TO THE READER.

THE bookworm who values his treasures for themselves alone, and thinks less of their pecuniary value than of their words; who loves to conjure up the spirits of those who yet speak in the printed pages, and shall perhaps live for all time in the lesson they have taught mankind, to trace their career, and to moralise on their end—such as he, and they are many, will not find their privacy intruded upon in this short essay. It would be an impertinence to seek to regulate their lives or to pry into their secrets.

Between them and the book-hunter there is a wide difference, so great that it might be impossible to bridge the gulf that divides them even if it were desirable to do so. The one lives in the past, the other is a man of action, and the two have little in common.

Ruskin says that "Bread of flour is good, but there is bread sweet as honey, if we would eat, in a good book ; nor is it serviceable until it has been read and re-read, and loved and loved again "—a sentiment that would certainly have been echoed by Southey, who, when his mind gave way, sat for hours at a time in his study handling and staring vacantly at his favourite books.

Nevertheless, the wayfarer who haunts the bookstalls, though he may be considered too much of the earth, earthy, by his more exclusive brother, has his pleasures also, and is by no manner of means a hunter and nothing more. His pride is none the less genuine because it is of the baser sort—or rather let us say, because it is not so punctilious. His pedigree also reaches back to the magician who earned his sinister title through the invention of an art which has revolutionised the world ; his hopes are truly eternal.

It is to him, and many like him, that the fore-going pages will appeal with greatest force ; and so I dismiss myself paraphrasing the words of a writer who, though more of a sportsman than a bookworm, was deeply tinged with the same spirit of anticipation that moves them both:

"Farewell, dear brothers of the chase, and when you go forth to take your pleasure either in the streets which roar with the traffic of the hurrying crowd or in the less noisy byways and alleys of the town, may your sport be ample and your hearts light. But should others prove more sagacious than yourselves—a circumstance, excuse me, that is by no means impossible; should they, alas!—but Fate avert it—reject your proffered overtures, the course of your steps will always lead you to pleasant places. In these we leave you to the quiet contemplation of the works of those who have gone before, whether it may be your pleasure to sally out when the spring lightens your task or in the more advanced season, when the flickering gas-jets preside over the scene."

FINIS.